Keeping *the* Faith

When Things Get Tough

Peter's Letter to Jesus Believers
Scattered Everywhere

*Bite-Size Studies Through
the Book of First Peter*

Jeff Doles

Keeping the Faith When Things Get Tough
© 2012 by Jeff Doles

All rights reserved. No part of this publication may be reproduced, stored in a retrieval system, or transmitted in any form or by any means—for example, electronic, photocopy, recording—without the prior written permission of the author.

Published by
Walking Barefoot Ministries
P.O. Box 1062, Seffner, FL 33583

ISBN: 978-0-9823536-2-2

All scripture quotations, unless otherwise indicated, are taken from the *New King James Version*. © 1982 by Thomas Nelson, Inc. Used by permission. All rights reserved.

Scripture quotations marked *NASB* are taken from the New American Standard Bible®, © The Lockman Foundation 1960, 1962, 1963, 1968, 1971, 1972, 1973, 1975, 1977, 1995. Used by permission. All rights reserved.

Scripture quotations marked *HCSB* are taken from the Holman Christian Standard Bible®, Copyright © 1999, 2000, 2002, 2003, 2009 by Holman Bible Publishers. All rights reserved.

Scripture taken from *The Message* by Eugene H. Peterson, © 1993, 1994, 1995, 1996, 2000. Used by permission of NavPress Publishing Group. All rights reserved.

Scripture quotations marked *ESV* are taken from The Holy Bible, English Standard Version, © 2001 by Crossway Bibles, a division of Good News Publishers. Used by permission. All rights reserved.

Cover foreground image: Saint Peter, a 6th-century encaustic icon from Saint Catherine's Monastery, Mount Sinai. Anonymous. Public domain. Cover background image: Passion altar, left inner panel, upper Scene: Kiss of Judas, by Hans Holbein the Younger. Public domain.

Cover design and book interior by *www.ChristianBookDesign.com*

For more resources on enjoying new life in Christ, living in faith and the power of the Holy Spirit, or to find out more about Jeff Doles, visit our websites:

www.WalkingBarefoot.com
www.TheFaithLog.com
www.JeffDoles.com

Contents

Introduction – Keep the Faith, Change the World 5

A Letter from Rocky 7

A Letter to Scatterlings 11

The Abundant Mercy of God Revealed in Jesus the Messiah 14

A Joy Words Cannot Contain 17

The Intense Desire of Prophets and Angels 20

New Birth, New Mind, New Life 22

The Destiny of Holiness 25

Living in Awe of the Redeemer God 26

The Gospel of Fervent Love 28

Incorruptible Seed, Incorruptible Harvest 31

Growing Up in New Life 34

Honored by God or Destined to Fall? 37

A New Kind of People 40

Glorifying God on the Day of Inspection 43

Living in True Freedom 46

Undermining Slavery with True Freedom 48

Transforming Marriages with True Freedom 51

A Life of Blessing 56

A Ready Heart and a Gentle Response   59

Suffering Messiah, Reigning King   62

Armed with the Attitude of Jesus   66

The End is Here?   69

Manifesting the Glory and Dominion of Jesus   72

An Unexpected Cause for Rejoicing   74

Deliverance in Difficult Times   77

Wearing the Victor's Crown   80

Clothing Yourself with Greatness   83

Under the Mighty Hand of God   86

Standing Firm Against the Adversary   88

The Grace of God in Which We Stand   90

Introduction ~
Keep the Faith, Change the World

When times are hard, it can be very tempting to hold on to the world and let go of the faith. The apostle Peter certainly knew what that was like when he denied Jesus three times, mere hours after pledging unshakeable faithfulness. However, with the reality of the resurrection and the power of the Holy Spirit, he learned how to do just the opposite—to keep the faith and change the world!

In his letter to Jesus believers who were scattered abroad and experiencing persecution and hardship, he reveals not only how to keep the faith in difficult circumstances but also how to change the world by the new life that comes from Jesus, a life of loving, giving and serving.

This book is a study of that letter. It comes from a series I taught on First Peter in the Bible study group I have lead for the past ten years. Teaching it live inspired me to expand on it in a series of posts at my blog (*www.TheFaithLog.com*). And now I have collected those posts together and edited them into this present form (I believe in "retasking").

These are "bite-size" studies to help guide you through Peter's letter a little at a time. For the most part, they retain the shape and style of the blog (minus all the typos). At the end of each study, I have added some focus questions to help you think further about the truths Peter brings. I have left them open-ended to allow for maximum personal reflection and group discussion.

My intent with this book, as with my blog, is to encourage you and stir up your faith to receive the wonderful promises and walk in the divine destiny God has for you. For many years now, my favorite verse, the one I come back to again and again, is Isaiah 50:4. "The Lord God has given me the tongue of disciples, that I may know how to sustain the weary one with a word. He awakens me morning by morning, He awakens my ear to listen as a disciple" (NASB). That has been my desire with this project and, indeed, with all my writing and ministry—to sustain the weary one with a word.

A Letter from Rocky

Peter, an apostle of Jesus Christ. (1Peter 1:1)

The name *Peter* comes from the Greek word, *petros*, which means "rock." It is the name Jesus gave Simon Bar-Jonah when he received a very important truth from God.

When Jesus came into the region of Caesarea Philippi, He asked His disciples, saying, "Who do men say that I, the Son of Man, am?"

So they said, "Some say John the Baptist, some Elijah, and others Jeremiah or one of the prophets."

He said to them, "But who do you say that I am?"

Simon Peter answered and said, "You are the Christ, the Son of the living God."

Jesus answered and said to him, "Blessed are you, Simon Bar-Jonah, for flesh and blood has not revealed this to you, but My Father who is in heaven. And I also say to you that you are Peter, and on this rock I will build My church, and the gates of Hades shall not prevail against it. And I will give you the keys of the kingdom of heaven, and whatever you bind on earth will be bound in heaven, and whatever you loose on earth will be loosed in heaven." (Matthew 16:13-19)

Simon did not come up with this on his own. It was a revelation he received directly from heaven. It was the sudden, divine realization that the one to whom he was speaking was the promised Messiah, the Anointed One who would deliver Israel and set the whole world right. It was the heaven-induced recognition that Jesus was not merely human but divine.

Jesus called him Rock because he had received this foundational truth. On this revelation, Jesus built His Church, and the "gates of hell"—even death itself—are not able to overcome it. Peter had found a rock to build his life upon, and now God would use him to lay that same foundation in others. That is how an apostle functions. An apostle is someone who is sent as the messenger and representative of another. As an apostle of Jesus the Messiah, he serves on behalf of Jesus. His function is to prepare the way, to break the ground, lay foundation. Paul speaks of the Church as being "built on the foundation of the apostles and prophets, Jesus Christ himself being the chief cornerstone" (Ephesians 2:20).

Now, Peter was an impetuous sort of person, not a very stable trait for a leader. He threw himself into whatever he did but was often in over his head, and sometimes his boldness left him stranded.

- He was the only disciple who, seeing Jesus walking on the waves, asked Him to bid him come (Matthew 14:28). That was bold. But he stepped out on the water and ended up sinking into the stormy sea because of his lack of faith (Matthew 14:30-31).
- On the other hand, he failed spectacularly! He was the only disciple willing to get out of the boat and, after all, he *did* walk on the water for at least a little while (Matthew 14:29).
- He was the one who boldly declared the revelation he received from the Father concerning Jesus the Messiah (Matthew 16:16).

- But just a few verses later, when Jesus spoke of being killed at the hands of elders and priests and scribes, Peter rebuked Him—rebuked the Messiah, the Son of the Living God!— saying, "Far be it from You, Lord; this shall not happen to You!" At this, Jesus said, "Get behind Me, Satan! You are an offense to Me, for you are not mindful of the things of God, but the things of men" (Matthew 16:20-23).
- On the night Jesus was betrayed, He said to the disciples, "All of you will be made to stumble because of Me this night." Peter audaciously answered, "Even if all are made to stumble because of You, I will never be made to stumble." Jesus answered, "Assuredly, I say to you that this night, before the rooster crows, you will deny Me three times" (Matthew 26:31-34), which is exactly what happened.
- On the third day, when the disciples received the report from Mary Magdalene, Peter was the only one who ran out with John to see the empty tomb (John 20:1-4).
- Fifty days later, at the feast of Pentecost in Jerusalem, where the Holy Spirit filled the disciples in the Upper Room, so that they all spoke with other tongues until observers accused them of being drunk, Peter stood up in the boldness of the Holy Spirit and proclaimed Jesus as Messiah and King (Acts 2).
- When Peter and John went up to pray at the temple and saw a lame man begging alms, Peter extended his faith and said, "Silver and gold I do not have, but what I do have I give you: In the name of Jesus Christ of Nazareth, rise up and walk," and the man was healed (Acts 3:1-10).
- Then when brought up before the magistrates, Peter declared, "Let it be known to you all, and to all the people of Israel, that by the name of Jesus Christ of Nazareth, whom you crucified, whom God raised from the dead, by Him this man stands here

before you whole" (Acts 4:10). And when admonished not to preach Jesus anymore, Peter and John answered, "Whether it is right in the sight of God to listen to you more than to God, you judge. For we cannot but speak the things which we have seen and heard" (Acts 4:19-20).

- ❧ Peter discerned the lie of Ananias and Sapphira and how satan filled their hearts. He was not afraid to call it what it was, and they both fell down dead (Acts 5:1-11).
- ❧ Brought before the council again for preaching the name of Jesus, Peter answered, "We ought to obey God rather than men," and did not relent (Acts 5:29).
- ❧ Peter broke ground for the preaching of the gospel to the nations, going to Cornelius, a Gentile, after receiving a vision from God (Acts 10).
- ❧ Then he stood before the leaders of the Church at Jerusalem and testified how God was making no distinction between Jews and Gentiles but was purifying both by faith in Jesus the Messiah (Acts 15).
- ❧ But then, it was also Peter whom Paul rebuked for hypocrisy at Antioch, when Peter backed away from fellowship with Gentile believers after a certain group of Jewish believers came from Jerusalem (Galatians 2:11-21).

Though his temperament at the beginning was "rocky" and tumultuous, God eventually smoothed him out and made him a pastor who was able to lay a good foundation for others and lead them to stability in Jesus Christ. Thirty years on from the Resurrection and Pentecost, Simon the Rock, writing in the AD 60s, now penned this letter of encouragement and instruction to converts going through difficult times of persecution where bold faith was required.

Focus Questions

1. What happened that brought Peter to a place of stability, boldness and follow-through in his faith?

2. Even after Peter was well into his ministry, he apparently still had moments of intimidation — at least one, when he backed away from table fellowship with Gentile believers because of a particular group from Jerusalem. and Paul rebuked him for it (see Galatians 2:11-21). Did that disqualify him from the ministry of apostle? Should it have?

3. What did Peter learn from that experience?

A Letter to Scatterlings

To the pilgrims of the Dispersion in Pontus, Galatia, Cappadocia, Asia, and Bithynia, elect according to the foreknowledge of God the Father, in sanctification of the Spirit, for obedience and sprinkling of the blood of Jesus Christ: Grace to you and peace be multiplied. (1 Peter 1:1-2)

Peter writes this from "Babylon" (1 Peter 5:13), which may be a code name for Rome. In the Old Testament, to which he frequently alludes, Babylon was the place of exile for the Jews, and Rome was quickly becoming a place of intense persecution for Jesus believers. Or this letter could possibly have been written from the city of Babylon, in the Egyptian delta (not the Babylon of Israel's ancient captivity). Persecuted Jews had long found refuge in Egypt, and many early Christians also ended up there. Mark, author of the book that largely represented Peter's account of the Gospel, established a church in Alexandria and was martyred there (see *The African Memory of Mark*, by Thomas Oden).

Peter writes to people who are "pilgrims," "temporary residents" (*HCSB*), "strangers" (*KJV*), "those who reside as aliens" (*NASB*), "exiles" (*ESV*). They were probably not actual exiles in the technical sense of being displaced from their homeland. But they had embraced faith in Jesus the Messiah, and with that a new way of life. Their true citizenship was, as Paul would say, in heaven (Philippians 3:20). They did not fit in with the surrounding culture and were consequently ostracized. Then, too, persecution of Jesus believers was heating up in Rome, under Nero, and news of it would have been reaching the outlying regions.

These believers were *diaspora*, scatterlings dispersed throughout five Romans provinces in Asia Minor, in what is now Turkey. The scattered ones James wrote his letter to were mostly Jewish believers, of the "twelve tribes," spread out among non-believing Gentiles (James 1:1). These to whom Peter writes are a blend of Gentile believers in Jesus, as well as some Jewish ones, who were displaced, geographically or socially, because of their faith in Jesus the Messiah.

Peter calls them "elect," chosen "according to the foreknowledge of God." They are the people of God and part of His eternal plan. Whatever they are going through, it has not taken God by surprise and, more importantly, He will not let them down but will see them through.

They are sanctified, consecrated, set apart by the Holy Spirit as God's own. It is why He has chosen them, to obey Jesus Christ and be sprinkled with His blood. This is an allusion to Exodus 24:7-8, when God first made covenant with the children of Israel. The people answered, "All that the LORD has said we will do, and be obedient." Then Moses took the blood of sacrifice and sprinkled it on them, saying, "This is the blood of the covenant which the LORD has made with you according to all these words." In Jesus the Messiah, we are joined to God in a new and better covenant, which is established on better promises (Hebrews 8:6). At the Last Supper, Jesus took the cup of wine and said, "This is the new covenant in My blood, which is shed for you" (Luke 22:20). The obedience here is the obedience of faith, committing ourselves to Jesus our Messiah.

Though Peter does not develop a theology of the Trinity here, notice how he identifies the three persons of the Godhead: the Father in His foreknowledge and gracious choice, Jesus the Messiah in the shedding of His blood, and the sanctifying work of the Holy Spirit.

Then there is the benediction, the words of blessing, "Grace to you and peace be multiplied." A common Jewish salutation was "Greetings and peace," but the apostles altered that. The Greek word for "greetings," *chairein*, means to be well and full of cheer. But the apostles used a related word, *charis*, the word for "grace." In their usage, it signifies the grace or favor that comes from God. The Greek word for "peace" is *eirene*, but being Jewish, Peter no doubt had in mind the Hebrew *shalom*, which speaks of the wholeness that comes from God. The addition of "be multiplied" is found only in Peter's letters and the epistle of Jude. It speaks of the fullness of divine favor and wholeness being revealed. God does not withhold His blessing from us, but as we grow in grace and come to know the Lord Jesus more and more (2 Peter 3:18), we experience more and more the fullness of His grace and peace.

This letter was to be copied and circulated especially to the churches in Pontus, Galatia, Cappadocia, Asia, and Bithynia, although it has, of course, come to the whole Church in the canon of Scripture.

Some commentators take it as a catechism, instruction for converts, or a letter of exhortation and encouragement for the newly baptized.

Focus Questions

1. How is it possible that a person can be chosen by God but persecuted in the world?

2. The Holy Spirit has set apart believers in Jesus as God's own people. In what ways does this manifest in the world?

3. Besides being a reference to the new covenant with God through Jesus, what might be another reason Paul speaks to these scattered believers of the "sprinkling of the blood of Jesus"?

The Abundant Mercy of God Revealed in Jesus the Messiah

Blessed be the God and Father of our Lord Jesus Christ, who according to His abundant mercy has begotten us again to a living hope through the resurrection of Jesus Christ from the dead, to an inheritance incorruptible and undefiled and that does not fade away, reserved in heaven for you, who are kept by the power of God through faith for salvation ready to be revealed in the last time. (1 Peter 1:3-5)

Peter uses a very Jewish form of prayer: "Blessed be God." The object of his praise is the One who is the Father of our Lord Jesus, in whom are fulfilled the promises of God to the patriarchs and prophets of the Old Testament. Jesus is King and Messiah for the sake of both Jewish and Gentile believers, and Peter, addressing both groups without distinction, calls Him *our* Lord.

In Jesus the Messiah, God has displayed His abundant mercy. Though writing in Greek, Peter would have most likely had the Hebrew word *hesed* in mind, the word used so often in the Old Testament for the faithful love and mercy God promised to show His covenant people. Peter then details some of the ways this divine love and mercy are revealed to us in the Lord Jesus.

- *Through the new birth.* God has begotten us again through faith in the Lord Jesus, so that we would have the right to become children of God (John 1:12). This new birth is from above, by the Spirit of God (John 3:3-6). We are born again of the Sprit but also of the incorruptible seed of the Word of God (1 Peter 1:23). God, who called the world into existence by His Word, gives us new birth by that same Word.
- *Through a living hope.* The biblical use of "hope" does not refer to wishful thinking or to things that are tentative. It speaks of a positive expectation, a joyful anticipation. In Jesus the Messiah, we have a *living* hope. It is the joyful anticipation of divine life and fellowship without end. In Ephesians, Paul prayed that God would give us wisdom and revelation by the Holy Spirit so that we would be able to know what this hope is all about (Ephesians 1:17-18).
- *Through the resurrection of Jesus the Messiah from the dead.* Here is the direct reason we have a living anticipation: Jesus has been raised from the dead. Paul calls Him "the firstborn from the dead" (Colossians 1:18) and spends a great deal of time in 1 Corinthians 15 talking about what that means for us who believe in Him. The

Jews expected that there would be a resurrection of the just at the end of the age, but in the resurrection of Jesus, the end of the age has broken into the midst of this present age as the firstfruits, the surety of what is to come for all who trust in Him.

- *Through an inheritance that is indestructible and undefiled.* Inheritance speaks of family and fatherhood. Through the new birth, we have God as our Father and are part of His family, heirs of God and joint heirs with Christ (Romans 8:17). In Adam, we inherited death and moral corruption (Romans 5). In Jesus the Messiah, we inherit life and purity. In his second letter, Peter says that God has given us "exceedingly great and precious promises, that through these you may be partakers of the divine nature, having escaped the corruption that is in the world through lust" (2 Peter 1:4). This inheritance will not fade away, as flowers do, but is carefully guarded for us in heaven. It is from heaven but it is not just for heaven, for in the resurrection, our life will be on earth, and heaven and earth will be finally and fully joined together as one (Revelation 21).

- *Through the coming revelation of salvation.* This is the ultimate unveiling of what God is doing in us. We enter into the family by faith in the Lord Jesus, and God is currently maturing the life of Jesus in us through work of the Holy Spirit. One day it shall all be revealed. John said, "Beloved, now we are children of God; and it has not yet been revealed what we shall be, but we know that when He is revealed, we shall be like Him, for we shall see Him as He is. And everyone who has this hope in Him purifies himself, just as He is pure" (1 John 3:2).

Focus Questions

1. Jesus believers have a living hope, a lively expectation through the resurrection of Jesus from the dead. What difference does that expectation mean for this present life?

2. Jesus believers have an incorruptible inheritance reserved in heaven. What are some ways this inheritance might be experienced in this present life?

3. Jesus believers "are kept by the power of God through faith for salvation ready to be revealed in the last time." In view of that, how should we live in this present time?

A Joy Words Cannot Contain

In this you greatly rejoice, though now for a little while, if need be, you have been grieved by various trials, that the genuineness of your faith, being much more precious than gold that perishes, though it is tested by fire, may be found to praise, honor, and glory at the revelation of Jesus Christ, whom having not seen you love. Though now you do not see Him, yet believing, you rejoice with joy inexpressible and full of glory, receiving the end of your faith—the salvation of your souls. (1 Peter 1:6-9)

"In this"—a new birth, a living hope, an incorruptible and unfading inheritance ready to be revealed—there is cause for great rejoicing. The Greek word behind "greatly rejoice" is *agalliao*, which literally means to "jump for joy." It is made up of two words: *agan*, which means "much" and *hallomai*, which means to leap, spring up or gush like water. It is not a joy that is quiet and sedate but one that is exuberant, ecstatic, animated.

What is more, it is a joy that will endure, even in the face of all the various, distressing trials that may test it. Such trials only reveal the genuineness of faith—not just faith as the act of believing, but faith as the object of our trust: Jesus the Messiah and the promise of God we have in Him.

Peter compares it to the refining of gold. There is a Jewish form of argument implied here, known as *qal vahomer*, arguing from the lesser to the greater. It is the kind of argument Jesus used when He said, "How much more ..." (e.g., Luke 11:13; Luke 12:24, 28). If gold, which can be destroyed, is considered valuable, then how much more precious is our faith, which will not only endure but will result in praise, honor and glory when King Jesus appears.

This is an apt comparison. When gold is refined, it is heated up until the dross (impurities) comes to the surface and is scooped away. Caution is required because if it is overheated, the gold will be destroyed—it will perish. The process is repeated until the gold is so pure the refiner can see his reflection in it.

Likewise, God allows trials to come in order to refine us. Not to destroy our faith but to remove the impurities that hinder our faith, for it is faith that overcomes the world and its present distresses (1 John 5:4). When God allows our faith to be "tested by fire," it is so we may reflect the Lord Jesus. As John says, "When He is revealed, we shall be like Him, for we shall see Him as He is. And everyone who has this hope in Him purifies himself, just as He is pure" (1 John 3:2). His glory will be revealed in us, and indeed, we will share in His glory, just as the moon shares in the glory of the sun by revealing it in the darkness. One day it will all be revealed in full, but it has already begun, even now.

Peter saw Jesus in the flesh, in His earthly ministry, but those to whom Peter writes had not, yet they loved Him anyway. The fact that they did not have the same natural experience of Jesus that Peter had did not matter one bit. They had the Holy Spirit *in* them to reveal the Lord Jesus *to* them and that was quite enough for them to fall in love with Him. Though they did not presently see him, they believed in Him anyway. Faith does not require sight! Paul said that "faith comes by hearing, and hearing by the Word of God" (Romans 10:17). The Holy Spirit takes the Word of God, the preaching of the good news about King Jesus the Messiah, and reveals Him to us.

Not only did they believe, they "rejoiced"—there's that word *agalliao* again—they "jumped for joy" because of Him. Not only joy that was exuberant and ecstatic, but "inexpressible and full of glory." It is a joy that words cannot contain, a joy that reveals the glory of God, a joy that makes present tests and trials pale by comparison.

It is a joy that lays hold of the result of our faith, the salvation of our souls. The Greek word for "salvation," *soteria*, means to rescue, preserve, prosper, restore to health and well-being. Peter has already spoken of it as something to be revealed (future tense) in the "last time," but here he speaks of already receiving it (present, continuous tense). The future is breaking into the present and we get to experience more and more as we overcome, through faith, the various trials of the present.

The Greek word for "receive" here, *komizo*, is about receiving what has been promised. In King Jesus the Messiah, we have received wonderful promises and we can begin to experience their fulfillment now in this time. Present distresses get swallowed up by the inexpressible joy of God's salvation already coming into the world.

Focus Questions

1. Why does God allow trials to come into the lives of Jesus believers?

2. How is His glory revealed in us through this process?

3. How is it possible to love, believe and have great joy in someone we have never seen?

The Intense Desire of Prophets and Angels

> *Of this salvation the prophets have inquired and searched carefully, who prophesied of the grace that would come to you, searching what, or what manner of time, the Spirit of Christ who was in them was indicating when He testified beforehand the sufferings of Christ and the glories that would follow. To them it was revealed that, not to themselves, but to us they were ministering the things which now have been reported to you through those who have preached the gospel to you by the Holy Spirit sent from heaven—things which angels desire to look into.* (1 Peter 1:10-12)

The prophets of the Old Testament spoke by the Holy Spirit, whom Peter here calls the Spirit of Messiah (Christ). They brought the promise of salvation, which has now been fulfilled by Jesus the Messiah and is being revealed to us. Though they brought the message, these prophets did not understand exactly how and when it would come about, but they longed to know. Peter uses three verbs to bring out the intensity of this desire:

- "inquired," Greek *ekzeteo*, the craving to know something, to thoroughly seek it out.
- "searching," Greek *ereuneo*, to investigate or examine.
- "searched diligently," *exereuneo*, an intensified form of eruneo.

Pairing together "inquired" (*ekzeteo*) with "searched diligently" (*exereuneo*)," as Peter does here, concentrates these already emphatic words even more. It is almost as if he cannot find enough words to show how much the Old Testament prophets longed to know the things Peter was now talking about. Earlier, he wrote of the intense, unmitigated, inexpressible joy we can now have in Jesus. Now, he reveals another dimension of that joy by describing the passionate longing of the prophets to know all about God's plan for us.

The Holy Spirit testified beforehand, witnessing to them in advance about the things that Messiah would suffer for the sake of God's people and the *glories* (note the plural) that would follow, and what this suffering would mean, not just for Israel, but for all the world. The prophets understood that these things would not be fulfilled in their own day but were for future generations. Peter says they were ministering to us to whom the gospel—the good news that Messiah has now come into the world—has been preached.

Peter knows very well when and why the Holy Spirit was "sent from heaven." He was there at Pentecost, when the Spirit of God descended upon Jesus' disciples. Before ascending to heaven, Jesus had promised, "You shall receive power when the Holy Spirit has come upon you; and you shall be witnesses to Me in Jerusalem, and in all Judea and Samaria, and to the end of the earth" (Acts 1:8). The same Spirit who foretold the coming of Messiah through the prophets now proclaimed it through Spirit-filled witnesses, of which Peter was one.

Peter then says something that lifts this wonder up even higher.

He has spoken of the great passion of the prophets to understand these things. Now he speaks of these as "things angels desire to look into." The Greek word for "desire" is *epithumeo*. It is made up of two words: *epi*, which here signifies intensity, and *thumeo*, which is passion. The word for "look" is *parakupto*, also made up of two words: *para*, beside and *kupto*, to bend forward or stoop down. Picture angels leaning over, stooping sideways, stretching their necks, with an intense curiosity, passion and awe to see the wonderful things God has done for us. *The Message* Bible says, "Angels would have given anything to be in on this!"

The prophets of old did not live to see these things come to pass. Angels are sort of bystanders, "ministering spirits sent forth to minister for those who will inherit salvation" (Hebrews 1:14). But we heirs of this promise. If prophets passionately sought to understand it and angels intensely desire to stoop low just to see it, how marvelous it must be for we who now receive it.

Focus Questions

1. What is the salvation the Old Testament prophets foretold?

2. How much did the prophets themselves understand about this salvation?

3. Why do angels so intensely desire to look into these things?

New Birth, New Mind, New Life

Therefore gird up the loins of your mind, be sober, and rest your hope fully upon the grace that is to be brought to you at the revelation of Jesus Christ; as obedient children, not conforming yourselves to the former lusts, as in your ignorance; but as He who called you is holy, you also be holy in all your conduct, because it is written, "Be holy, for I am holy." (1 Peter 1:13-16)

"Therefore"—because of the new birth, the living hope, the incorruptible inheritance and inexpressible joy we have in Jesus— "gird up the loins of your mind." The mind, of course, has no loins. "Girding the loins" is a metaphor for preparing for action. The robes worn in Peter's day could be gathered up for one to move quickly and easily. "Prepare your mind for actions" is how the *NASB* puts it. Or as *The Message* says, "Put your mind in gear."

Peter wants believers to be prepared to think in a new way because of what God is revealing *to* us and *in* us. Paul speaks similarly in Romans 12:2, "Do not be conformed to this world, but be transformed by the renewing of your mind, that you may prove what is that good and acceptable and perfect will of God." Both Peter and Paul tell us that we need to renew our thinking with the truth of the gospel.

"Be sober," Peter says, or "sober-minded" (*ESV*), or "sober in spirit" (*NASB*). He is talking about being directed by this new way of thinking. We are to set our hope, our expectation, on the grace, the favor of God that brings us this salvation, which will come to its completion when Jesus is revealed at the end of the age, and we shall be like Him, for we shall see Him as He is (1 John 3:2).

"As obedient children." Through faith in Jesus the Messiah, we receive new birth and become children of God. The Greek word for "obedience" comes from a root, *hypakouo*, which has to do with hearing. As children of God, we are to give heed to a new voice. "Not conforming yourselves to the former lusts, as in your ignorance." Conformity speaks of our outward manner of life. Before we knew God, we were left to our own corrupt desires. But these no longer match the inward reality of who we now are in Jesus. As Paul said in Romans 12:2, we are not to be *conformed* but *transformed*, so that our outward manner corresponds to our inner being, our new life in Messiah.

Peter says the same thing as Paul, only in a different way: "But as He who called you is holy, you also be holy in all your conduct, because it is written, 'Be holy, for I am holy.'" God has called us and it is now His voice we are to listen to. Our manner of life is to reflect what He is like—we can do that now because of our new life in Jesus. God is "holy," which means that He is set apart; there is no one else like Him in all the world. We, too, are holy, which means that we are set apart as God's own, and our lives should demonstrate that. Paul speaks of the fruit of the Spirit: love, joy, peace, longsuffering, kindness, goodness, faithfulness, gentleness, self-control (Galatians 5:22-23), the work of God's Spirit to bring forth the character of Jesus the Messiah in our lives.

Focus Questions

1. What are the new ways of thinking we are to embrace because of the new birth, the living hope and the incorruptible inheritance we have in Jesus?

2. When Jesus is revealed at the end of the age, the favor of God will bring His salvation work to completion. What should our lives like as we set our expectation on that?

3. What does it mean to be holy? ? Is being holy different from doing "holy" things?

The Destiny of Holiness

Because it is written, "Be holy, for I am holy." (1 Peter 1:16)

Both the Hebrew and Greek words for "holy" mean to be set apart. In the Scriptures, being made holy, or sanctified, means to be set aside for God's special purposes. Some people think of holiness as a somber and dour thing. But I tell you that it is a joyful thing, full of awe and wonder. For holiness speaks of divine destiny and purpose—a fellowship, a partnership with God.

Now, understand that you and I could never set ourselves apart for God's purposes. It is something He must do for us. But that is what the grace of God is all about and why Jesus came. He said to the Father, "Behold, I have come to do Your will, O God." It is by that will, the author of Hebrews says, that we have been sanctified—made holy—through the offering of the body of Jesus the Messiah once for all (Hebrews 10:10).

God sets us apart by the offering of His Son, but also by the truth of His Word. As Jesus prayed, "Sanctify them by Your truth. Your Word is truth" (John 17:17).

So Peter exhorts us, not to try and make ourselves holy, but to live according to the holiness by which God has already set us apart in the Lord Jesus. It is living according to the truth of His Word, according to the life of Jesus that now dwells in us. As Paul said,

I have been crucified with Christ; it is no longer I who live, but

> *Christ lives in me; and the life which I now live in the flesh I live by faith in the Son of God, who loved me and gave Himself for me.* (Galatians 2:20)

Holiness is partaking of the divine nature:

> *His divine power has given to us all things that pertain to life and godliness, through the knowledge of Him who called us by glory and virtue, by which have been given to us exceedingly great and precious promises, that thought these you may be partakers of the divine nature, having escaped the corruption that is in the world through lust.* (2 Peter 1:3-4)

It is a call to step up into the life of divine destiny, to be who we really are in Jesus the Messiah.

Are you ready to embrace this holy calling and step up into the life of divine nature and fellowship? To live according to the faith and power of the King Jesus the Messiah? That is destiny indeed.

Focus Questions

1. To be holy is to be "set apart." In what way is God set apart?

2. For what purpose has God set *us* apart.

3. How does God fulfill that purpose in us.

Living in Awe of the Redeemer God

And if you call on the Father, who without partiality judges according to each one's work, conduct yourselves throughout the time of your stay here in fear; knowing that you were not redeemed with corruptible things, like silver or gold, from your aimless conduct received by tradition from your fathers, but with the precious blood of Christ, as of a lamb without blemish and without spot. He indeed was foreordained before the foundation of the world, but was manifest in these last times for you who through Him believe in God, who raised Him from the dead and gave Him glory, so that your faith and hope are in God. (1 Peter 1:17-21)

Peter continues the exhortation he began in verse 13, addressing believers who were aware of themselves as being sojourners in a foreign land. But they are children of God, born anew, who possess the inheritance of the Father. God is a father who discerns and distinguishes between works but not between persons—Peter had long ago learned that there was no difference to God between Jewish and Gentile believers. His judgment is not that of an angry, distant deity, but that of a good father. This calls for living with a "deep consciousness of God" (*The Message*), or as it is called in the Old Testament, the "fear of the LORD." It is not cringing in terror but living in respect and awe of God.

This was a new kind of living for them. Peter contrasts this with their old way of life. Before, they had lived according to the traditions they inherited from their fathers. Gentile believers came from pagan backgrounds that promoted immoral conduct and the worship of idols that could never save them. Jewish traditions had some problems of their own, developing attitudes and practices that made for a good outward show but could not deal with the problem of the heart.

Now they had been redeemed from those old, futile ways. The Greek word for "redeemed" refers to a ransom or the purchase price for the freedom of a slave. Here it is used of those who have been ransomed or delivered from bondage, not by silver or gold, but by a much higher price—the blood of Messiah. God planned this from the beginning, even before the creation of the world, knowing that our redemption would be necessary. But now it has been revealed in "these last times," a period that is signaled by the resurrection of Jesus from the dead and will continue until He comes again.

The resurrection changes everything, giving us new expectation, new life and a glory in which all those who trust in Jesus will have a share. God has raised the Lord Jesus from the dead and through Him, we believe in God, from whom we now receive everything good.

Focus Questions

1. What does the "fear of the LORD" mean to you?

2. How does the "fear of the LORD" differ from the way of life promoted by the surrounding culture today?

3. How does your life demonstrate faith and expectation in God?

The Gospel of Fervent Love

Since you have purified your souls in obeying the truth through the Spirit in sincere love of the brethren, love one another fervently with a pure heart, having been born again, not of corruptible seed but incorruptible, through the word of God which lives and abides forever, because "All flesh is as grass, and all the glory of man as the flower of the grass. The grass withers, and its flower falls away, but the word of the Lord endures forever." Now this is the word which by the gospel was preached to you. (1 Peter 1:22-25)

"Obeying the truth" is believing the truth about Jesus the Messiah and living according to it. It has a purifying effect on the soul. James said, "Be doers of the word, and not hearers only, deceiving yourselves" (James 1:22). This leads to "pure and undefiled religion before God ... to visit orphans and widows in their trouble, and to keep oneself unspotted from the world" (James 1:27). In other words, believing and doing the truth about Jesus teaches us how to live by teaching us how to love.

This is real, true love Peter is talking about. The Greek word for "sincere" is *anypokritos*, which is made up a two parts: *a* or *an*, which means "not," and *hypocritos*, which means "actor," as in a play, and is where we get our word "hypocrite." It is not pretending to love, wearing it as a mask or disguise, or reading lines as actors. As the apostle John tells us, "My little children, let us not love in word or in tongue, but in deed and in truth" (1 John 3:18).

Our love must be authentic but it must also be fervent. The Greek word for "fervent" is *ektenos*, from two words: *ek*, "out," and *teino*, "to stretch." It is "a constant concern to be of service, exacting and untiring zeal, urgent affection, and even lavish gift-giving" (Ceslas Spicq, *Theological Lexicon of the New Testament*). It is fervent because it comes from the heart. It is not a mere outward conformity but reveals an inward transformation.

Because these believers were being ostracized by a society that did not understand their faith or their way of life, it became all the more important for them to love each other with an intense devotion that reveals the new birth we have together in Jesus. Indeed, this new birth, and the inward transformation it brings, enables such love. That is because the new birth does not come from the seed of fallen humanity, which is subject to death and corruption, but by the seed of the Word of God, the Word of Life that endures forever. At this point, Peter quotes Isaiah 40:6-8, also written to exiles, about the brevity of human life in contrast to the eternality of the divine word.

> *The voice said, "Cry out!"*
> *And he said, "What shall I cry?"*
> *"All flesh is grass,*
> *And all its loveliness is like the flower of the field.*
> *The grass withers, the flower fades,*
> *Because the breath of the* LORD *blows upon it;*
> *Surely the people are grass.*
> *The grass withers, the flower fades,*
> *But the word of our God stands forever."*

This is from a messianic passage about God setting things right in the world and it finds its fulfillment in the Lord Jesus. Indeed, Peter takes the good news of Jesus the Messiah to be the same enduring word Isaiah described: "Now *this* is the word which by the gospel was preached to you."

Peter uses two different Greek words for "word" in this passage. The first is *logos*, which is the Word of God in general principle. The second is *rhema*, which is the Word of God acutely articulated, for example, through preaching. What was foretold by Isaiah in prophecy now finds acute fulfillment in the message of the gospel.

The gospel is what Peter has been talking about all along: The abundant mercy of God revealed in Jesus the Messiah, through the new birth, a living hope, and an incorruptible inheritance because of the resurrection of Jesus from the dead and faith in Him. It is the gospel of fervent love—God's love for us resulting in our love for each other.

Focus Questions

1. How does God's love for us teach us to love each other?

2. How is God's love for you being expressed in your love for others?

3. Why is it important that the word of God is incorruptible, indestructible, lasts forever?

Incorruptible Seed, Incorruptible Harvest

Having been born again, not of corruptible seed but incorruptible, through the word of God which lives and abides forever. (1 Peter 1:23)

This new birth that Peter speaks of does not come about by any human agency, for that would be corruptible seed. Rather, it comes from incorruptible seed and is divine in nature. The Word of God, which lives and abides forever, is that seed.

The Word of God is the manifestation of God, expressing His will, His desires and His purposes. Though it is presented us in the form of the written word, the Scriptures, it is preeminently revealed to us in Jesus the Messiah, the Word who has always been with God, and indeed is God, and who "became flesh and dwelt among us" (John 1:1, 14). It is this Word that John spoke about when he said,

> *As many as received Him, to them He gave the right to become children of God, to those who believe in His name; who were born, not of blood, nor of the will of the flesh, nor of the will of man, but of God (John 1:12-13)*

This is indeed incorruptible seed. In fact, it is God-seed.

Orange seeds produce orange trees which bring forth oranges that contain more orange seeds. Apple trees produce apple trees which bring forth apples that contain more apple seeds. As the seed is, so is the tree and its fruit—they possess the essential nature of the seed because they are "born" of the seed.

The seed by which we have been born again to eternal life is a divine seed, the Word of God—the Lord Jesus and all that God has spoken. It is "living and powerful" (Hebrews 4:12). This seed has been sown in us to bring forth the life of God, His divine nature, in us.

> *His divine power has given to us all things that pertain to life and godliness, through the knowledge of Him who called us by glory and virtue, by which have been given to us exceedingly great and precious promises, that, through these you may be* partakers of the divine nature, *having escaped the corruption that is in the world through lust. (2 Peter 1:3-4)*

This does not imply that we can ever become God Himself, but it does mean that we become *like* God in some very real and important aspects, just as man was originally created to be in His image and likeness (Genesis 1:26-27). We see this, for example, when Paul talks about the fruit of the Spirit: love, joy, peace, longsuffering, kindness, goodness, faith, gentleness and self-control (Galatians 5:22-23). These things reflect the character of God in Jesus the Messiah, and in all who are born of that incorruptible seed.

> *Whoever has been born of God does not sin, for His seed remains in him; and he cannot sin, because he has been born of God. (1 John 3:9)*

This divine essence is who we really are now in Jesus. Once we were dead in trespasses and sins, living according to the lusts of our flesh, "fulfilling the desires of the flesh and of the mind, and were by nature children of wrath" (Ephesians 2:1, 3). But now, because we have been born of incorruptible seed, we no longer have to submit to that. We can now do as Paul says, "Reckon yourselves to be dead indeed to sin, but alive to God in Christ Jesus our Lord" (Romans 6:11).

Focus Questions

1. How does the word of God reveal the will of God?

2. What is the relationship between Jesus and the Scriptures?

3. How are we born again by the incorruptible word of God?

Growing Up in New Life

Therefore, laying aside all malice, all deceit, hypocrisy, envy, and all evil speaking, as newborn babes, desire the pure milk of the word, that you may grow thereby, if indeed you have tasted that the Lord is gracious. (1Peter 2:1-3)

The old life with its old ways must be set aside; the new has come. These to whom Peter writes are not just born again, they are *newly* born again—babes! That is one reason why some commentators think this letter is a sort of catechism or a sermon to recently baptized believers.

There are certain things that must be put aside; they do not belong to the new life we have in Jesus the Messiah. The Greek word for "lay aside" is found elsewhere in the New Testament in similar contexts in which the apostles exhort believers:

The night is far spent, the day is at hand. Therefore let us cast off *the works of darkness, and let us put on the armor of light. Let us walk properly, as in the day, not in revelry and drunkenness, not in lewdness and lust, not in strife and envy. But put on the Lord Jesus Christ, and make no provision for the flesh, to fulfill its lusts. (Romans 13:12-13)*

Put off, *concerning your former conduct, the old man which grows corrupt according to the deceitful lusts, and be renewed in the spirit of your mind, and that you put on the new man which was created according to God, in true righteousness and holiness. (Ephesians 4:22-24)*

But now you yourselves are to put off *all these: anger, wrath, malice,*

> blasphemy, filthy language out of your mouth. Do not lie to one another, since you have put off the old man with his deeds, and have put on the new man who is renewed in knowledge according to the image of Him who created him. (Colossians 3:8-10)

> Therefore lay aside *all filthiness and overflow of wickedness, and receive with meekness the implanted word, which is able to save your souls.* (James 1:21)

Notice, though, that it is not enough to put all these things *off.* There must also be something that is *put on.* We are to put on the new man we have become in Jesus the Messiah, wearing now the life of Jesus as our own—because it now is our own! This involves a renewal in our way of thinking. It is not merely an outward conformity to the life of Jesus, but a transformation that reveals outwardly what is true of us inwardly. How does this happen? James tells us to "receive with meekness the implanted word." The Greek word for "receive" here means to take up or lay hold of. The "implanted" word is the word that was sown, like a seed, in the heart.

Peter spoke earlier of being "born again of incorruptible seed by the word of God." Now he tells these new believers to "desire the pure milk of the word." The phrase "of the word" translates the Greek word logicon, but it can just as well be rendered as "spiritual," that is, to desire "pure spiritual milk" as the *ESV, NIV* and other versions have it.

The word for "pure" here is *adolos* and stands in contrast to the word for "deceit" in verse 1, *dolos.* The *a* in front of it is an alpha-privative, a negative prefix. Its use in front of *dolos* means "without," that is, without deceit. The spiritual milk that Peter is talking about is pure, not mixed up with or contaminated by any additive. It is completely as it appears to be and is not a disguise for something else.

Peter continues the metaphor with, "if you have tasted that the Lord is gracious." This is a reference to Psalm 34:8, "Oh, taste and see that the LORD is good." The word for "gracious" here is not the word we normally expect, *charis*, but *chrestos*, which speaks of virtue, goodness, kindness. Notice that it is very similar to the Greek word for Messiah, *Christos*. Peter may be making a play on words here, because when he says "the Lord is gracious," he is referring to Jesus.

"Taste" speaks of an experience. Those who have believed in Jesus the Messiah have received the new birth and experienced the goodness and kindness of God. When you have tasted something good, it stimulates your appetite for more of the same. That is what Peter is getting at here: Since you have tasted the goodness of the Lord, let that stimulate your desire for more of Him, more of this spiritual food, more of the message about King Jesus. This is the "milk" by which we grow up in this new life in Him.

Make no mistake, there is a *process* of growth. Nobody is born fully mature, not in the physical realm nor in the spiritual. Having been discipled for so long by the way the world thinks and acts, we need to learn how to think in new ways, about who we are in Jesus, so that we may begin to walk out this new life we have received from God in Him.

Focus Questions

1. Peter tells us to lay aside all malice, deceit, hypocrisy, envy and insulting language. What might he tell us to put on instead?

2. How does the "pure spiritual milk" (the teaching about Jesus) help us put on the things we ought to put on?

3. Why did God make spiritual maturity a process of growth rather than an instant event?

Honored by God or Destined to Fall?

Coming to Him as to a living stone, rejected indeed by men, but chosen by God and precious, you also, as living stones, are being built up a spiritual house, a holy priesthood, to offer up spiritual sacrifices acceptable to God through Jesus Christ. Therefore it is also contained in the Scripture, "Behold, I lay in Zion a chief cornerstone, elect, precious, and he who believes on Him will by no means be put to shame." Therefore, to you who believe, He is precious; but to those who are disobedient, "The stone which the builders rejected has become the chief cornerstone," and "A stone of stumbling and a rock of offense." They stumble, being disobedient to the word, to which they also were appointed. (1 Peter 2:4-8)

Peter speaks of Jesus as a living stone, one rejected by men, but chosen and honored by God (the Greek word for "precious" means to be highly valued and esteemed). Then he goes further and speaks of believers as living stones. Jesus is the chief foundation stone God has laid for a spiritual house and we, as living stones, are together being built up as that house. We are also a holy priesthood, to offer up spiritual sacrifices in that spiritual house. Just as the Lord Jesus is accepted and established by God, so we, too, are accepted by God, because we are in Jesus. The spiritual house Peter describes is a temple. Throughout the Bible, the temple is the dwelling place of God, the place where heaven and earth come together. As those who have come to Jesus, then, we have become the place where God dwells on earth, the place where heaven and earth meet.

Quoting from Isaiah 28:16, "Behold, I lay in Zion a stone for a foundation, a tried stone, a precious cornerstone, a sure foundation,"

Peter highlights the connection between Jesus and those who believe in Him: "He who believes in Him will by no means be put to shame." Those who believe in Messiah, though they be rejected by men, are accepted by God. They will not be put to shame but will be honored by Him. The *NKJV* has 1 Peter 2:7 as, "To you who believe, *He is* precious." However, the words "He is" are italicized to indicate that they do not have an actual basis in the text but are supplied by the translator. The *ESV* offers a better translation: "So the honor is for you who believe." (This is supported by the *HCSB, NASB, Young's Literal Translation, Weymouth's New Testament* and other versions; also by *Robertson's Word Pictures, Vincent's Word Studies* and other expository works.)

Though Jesus is rejected by some, it does not change the truth about who He is. He remains the chief cornerstone, chosen and honored by God. At this point, Peter brings out Psalm 118:22, "The stone which the builders rejected has become the chief cornerstone." This is an important theme for him. When he was hauled before the Sanhedrin to explain himself—"By what power or by what name have you done this?"—Peter identified the power and name of Jesus the Messiah, and alluded to this verse very pointedly:

> *This is the "stone which was rejected by you builders, which has become the chief cornerstone." Nor is there salvation in any other, for there is no other name under heaven given among men by which we must be saved. (Acts 4:11-12)*

Jesus used this same passage to identify Himself in the Parable of the Wicked Vinedressers (Matthew 21:42; Mark 12:10; Luke 20:17), in which they expelled the King's son from the vineyard and killed him. Jesus asked, "Therefore what will the owner of the vineyard do to them? He will come and destroy those vinedressers and give the vineyard to others." The chief priests, scribes and Pharisees, recognizing themselves in that parable protested, "Certainly not!" Then Jesus looked directly at them and said, "What then is this that is written: 'The stone which the builders rejected has become the chief cornerstone'? Whoever falls on that stone will be broken; but on whomever it falls, it will grind him to powder" (Luke 20:15-18).

Peter adds another Scripture into the mix, a line from Isaiah 8:14. The stone which the builders rejected, which turned out to be the chief cornerstone, has become "a stone of stumbling and a rock of offence." To those who reject Jesus and refuse to receive Him as Messiah and King, the rock that should have been a sure foundation for them has become a judgment. "They stumble," Peter says, "being disobedient to the word, to which they also were appointed." There is only one chief cornerstone, and God knew all along that some would reject Him. Those who do are destined to stumble and fall.

Focus Questions

1. The theme of "chief cornerstone," first found in the Old Testament, occurs a number of times in the New Testament. What is the significance, and why is it so important?

2. What honor does faith in Jesus, the Chief Cornerstone, bring?

3. The house that is being built, of which Jesus is the Cornerstone, is a temple. What significance does this hold in regard to the kingdom of God.

A New Kind of People

> *But you are a chosen generation, a royal priesthood, a holy nation, His own special people, that you may proclaim the praises of Him who called you out of darkness into His marvelous light; who once were not a people but are now the people of God, who had not obtained mercy but now have obtained mercy.* (1 Peter 2:9-10)

Those who refused to believe the good news of God's Messiah, Peter said, were destined to stumble and fall. Then he turns to the believers. "But you ..." he says, and offers them words that speak of an amazing identity in Jesus the Messiah.

- *You are a chosen generation.* The Greek word for "generation" here is *genos*, which means "race" or "kind." The word for "chosen" is *eklekton*, "select" (this is where we get our word "eclectic"). God has selected a new kind of people, not based on biological characteristics or geographical or national boundaries but on the basis of faith in Jesus the Messiah. All who believe in Him, whether Jews or Gentiles (non-Jews, pagans, the nations) are part of this new people.
- *You are a royal priesthood.* God's plan for Israel was that she be a royal priesthood (Exodus 19:6), to come before God, not only for her own sake but also for the sake of the nations. But Israel failed in this task. Now this purpose is fulfilled in a way that Israel did not expect, through Jesus the Messiah, with Him as our High Priest.
- *You are a holy nation.* God also chose Israel to be a holy nation (Exodus 19:6), set apart especially for Him. Now He has enlarged that nation with believers from every nation. In Revelation, the song of praise sung to the Lamb of God is, "You are worthy to take the scroll, and to open its seals; for You were slain, and have

redeemed us to God by Your blood out of every tribe and tongue and people and nation, and have made us kings and priests to our God; and we shall reign on the earth" (Revelation 5:9-10). What good news for those who found themselves scattered among the nations and under their heel.

- *You are His own special people.* The Greek word is *peripoiesis*, which comes from two words: *peri*, "around," and *poieo*, to make or do. Put together, it means "to make around oneself." It is used speak of what one acquires or bring into possession for himself. God has redeemed us, purchased us at great price from bondage to sin and death, and gathered us around Himself.

Now Peter speaks of purpose: "That you may proclaim the praises of Him who called you out of darkness into His marvelous light." The word for "praise" here actually speaks of the virtues and excellencies of God. We proclaim his mercy and goodness. Before He ascended to His throne in heaven, Jesus told His disciples to wait in Jerusalem:

> *You shall receive power when the Holy Spirit has come upon you; and you shall be witnesses to Me in Jerusalem, and in all Judea and Samaria, and to the end of the earth. (Acts 1:8)*

> *Go into all the world and preach the gospel to every creature. He who believes and is baptized will be saved; but he who does not believe will be condemned. And these signs will follow those who believe: In My name they will cast out demons; they will speak with new tongues; they will take up serpents; and if they drink anything deadly, it will by no means hurt them; they will lay hands on the sick, and they will recover. (Mark 16:15-18)*

God wants this good news, the word of His glory revealed in Jesus the Messiah, to be spread all over earth, even in the realms of heaven.

To me, who am less than the least of all the saints, this grace was given, that I should preach among the Gentiles the unsearchable riches of Christ, and to make all see what is the fellowship of the mystery, which from the beginning of the ages has been hidden in God who created all things through Jesus Christ; to the intent that now the manifold wisdom of God might be made known by the church to the principalities and powers in the heavenly places, according to the eternal purpose which He accomplished in Christ Jesus our Lord. (Ephesians 3:8-11)

God shows His goodness and grace, not only *to* us, but also *through* us.

- He has called us out of darkness into His marvelous light.
- Once we were not a people, now we are the people of God.
- Once we had not received mercy, now we have received the mercy of God.

The last two points are a reference to Hosea 1:9-10 and 2:23, which originally described unbelieving Israel. Though they broke covenant with God, He would restore them as His people once again and show them mercy. Now through faith in Jesus the Messiah, both Israel and the nations are being restored to God as a new kind of people.

Focus Questions

1. What is the significance of God's chosen generation in the world?

2. What is the role of a priesthood?

3. How is this role fulfilled by the Church?

Glorifying God on the Day of Inspection

Beloved, I beg you as sojourners and pilgrims, abstain from fleshly lusts which war against the soul, having your conduct honorable among the Gentiles, that when they speak against you as evildoers, they may, by your good works which they observe, glorify God in the day of visitation. (1 Peter 2:11-12)

Peter continues his exhortation in a tender and personal way, addressing his readers as, "Beloved." Though they are resident aliens, they must be careful to abstain from "fleshly lusts," the passions of fallen human nature. These are not neutral or inconsequential but work against us. *The Message* renders it this way, "Don't indulge your ego at the expense of your soul." The apostle Paul draws the contrast between the lusts of the flesh and the fruit God wants to produce in us by His Spirit:

I say then: Walk in the Spirit, and you shall not fulfill the lust of the flesh. For the flesh lusts against the Spirit, and the Spirit against the flesh; and these are contrary to one another, so that you do not do the things that you wish. But if you are led by the Spirit, you are not under the law. Now the works of the flesh are evident, which are: adultery, fornication, uncleanness, lewdness, idolatry, sorcery, hatred, contentions, jealousies, outbursts of wrath,

> *selfish ambitions, dissensions, heresies, envy, murders, drunkenness, revelries, and the like; of which I tell you beforehand, just as I also told you in time past, that those who practice such things will not inherit the kingdom of God. (Galatians 5:16-21)*

Now look at what the Holy Spirit is working to bring forth in us:

> *But the fruit of the Spirit is love, joy, peace, longsuffering, kindness, goodness, faithfulness, gentleness, self-control. Against such there is no law. And those who are Christ's have crucified the flesh with its passions and desires. If we live in the Spirit, let us also walk in the Spirit. (Galatians 5:22-25)*

The Spirit of God wants to bring forth in us the life and character of Jesus the Messiah. This is the sort of excellent behavior and honorable conduct Peter has in mind. Part of the difficulty these scattered believers were experiencing was that the surrounding Gentiles did not understand what this faith in Jesus was all about. Jews were often slandered by Gentiles, and now those Gentiles who began to believe in the Messiah were experiencing similar slander.

Gentiles thought Christians were atheists because they did not bow to any of the pagan idols; that they were not good citizens because they proclaimed that Jesus, not Caesar, is the divine King; that they were cannibals because they spoke of eating the body of Jesus and drinking His blood (at the Table of the Lord). Gentiles were also critical of Christians because they upset the institutions of marriage, family and slavery by giving women, wives, children and slaves new dignity. The Christian message also undermined lucrative pagan practices such as temple prostitution and the market for idols.

Peter's answer to that was to live a noble lifestyle of love and good works. He knew the Gentiles would be "observing"—the Greek word means that they would be watching, carefully inspecting how these believers in Jesus lived. His expectation was that, by being good citizens, good servants, good husbands and wives, and having love for all, their manner as well as their message would cause their Gentile neighbors to give glory to God. This echoes what Jesus preached: "In the same way, let your light shine before men, so that they may see your good works and give glory to your Father in heaven" (Matthew 5:16).

What Peter especially has in mind here is that the Gentiles might glorify God "in the day of visitation." The Greek word for "visitation," *episcope*, signifies oversight, investigation, inspection. Peter is talking about the day of inspection, when God comes to set things right—judgment day! As the Gentiles inspected the lives if Christians, perhaps it would cause them to turn to Jesus the Messiah, so that on the day they were inspected by God, they would gladly give Him glory.

Focus Questions

1. How do "fleshly lusts" war against the soul?

2. Many of these were things the non-believing Gentiles practiced (sexual immoralities, for example). Why would believers abstaining from them cause the non-believers to glorify God?

3. The Old Testament law was never enough to control human behavior. How does Peter expect Jesus believers will be able to refrain from such lusts?

Living in True Freedom

> *Therefore submit yourselves to every ordinance of man for the Lord's sake, whether to the king as supreme, or to governors, as to those who are sent by him for the punishment of evildoers and for the praise of those who do good. For this is the will of God, that by doing good you may put to silence the ignorance of foolish men—as free, yet not using liberty as a cloak for vice, but as bondservants of God. Honor all people. Love the brotherhood. Fear God. Honor the king. (1 Peter 2:13-17)*

The first line, "Submit yourselves to every ordinance of man," can also be translated, as *Young's Literal Translation* has it, "Be subject, then, to every human creation," or even as "every human creature" (*The Expositor's Bible Commentary*, Vol. 12, p. 233). That would, of course, include every governing authority, but Peter may have something much bigger in mind than just those authorities. If we are to submit to "every human creature," then Peter levels the playing field: Yes, we are to submit ourselves to kings and governors, but more than that, we are to understand that we are here for the sake of everyone, not just rulers. We are here to serve whoever we come across.

Jesus the Messiah is King over all, but God has allowed governments and authorities to be instituted by men. Their rightful purpose, in God's plan, is to punish those who do evil and commend those who do good. We are to submit to those institutions and ordinances, but only in doing good, never in doing evil.

The Greek word used for "doing good," *agathapoieo*, includes moral virtue, but refers, more specifically, to doing what benefits others. Not just for those who do good things for us, but as Jesus taught, "Love your enemies, do good, and lend, hoping for nothing in return" (Luke 6:35). It is the good that flows from love. The apostle John said, "Beloved, do not imitate what is evil, but what is good. He who does good is of God, but he who does evil has not seen God" (3 John 11). Just as God loved the world and gave His Son (John 3:16), and Jesus came to serve and to give His life as a ransom for many (Mark 10:45), we are called to love and serve others. It is this kind of selfless giving that will help clear up misapprehensions about who we are and silence our critics.

As servants of God, we are free from everything else. However, God does not give us this freedom as a license to do evil but as the liberty to do good. Paul said, "Reckon yourselves to be dead indeed to sin, but alive to God in Christ Jesus our Lord" (Romans 6:11). Once we were in bondage to sin and our own base desires. Now we are free in Jesus the Messiah, and it is in loving God and serving others that we truly experience our freedom. Peter summarizes it this way:

- *Honor all people.* We are to treat everyone with dignity and respect.
- *Love the brotherhood.* We are to love, in particular, our brothers and sisters in the faith. Paul said, "Therefore, as we have opportunity, let us do good to all, especially to those who are of the household of faith" (Galatians 6:10).
- *Fear God.* We are to live in awe, respect and love for God. This will be evident in how we treat others. John said, "If someone says, 'I love God,' and hates his brother, he is a liar; for he who does not love his brother whom he has seen, how can he love God whom he has not seen?" (1 John 4:20).
- *Honor the king.* Jesus said, "Render to Caesar the things that are Caesar's, and to God the things that are God's" (Mark 12:17). The king is to be honored, but God alone is to be feared.

Focus Questions

1. What does it mean for a believer to live in true freedom?

2. Human governing authorities can often be tyrannical and oppressive. How might submitting to them in doing good bring about change in those authorities?

3. What does it mean to "honor the king"? What does it *not* mean?

Undermining Slavery with True Freedom

> *Servants, be submissive to your masters with all fear, not only to the good and gentle, but also to the harsh. For this is commendable, if because of conscience toward God one endures grief, suffering wrongfully. For what credit is it if, when you are beaten for your faults, you take it patiently? But when you do good and suffer, if you take it patiently, this is commendable before God. For to this you were called, because Christ also suffered for us, leaving us an example, that you should follow His steps: "Who committed no sin, nor was deceit found in His mouth"; who, when He was reviled, did not revile in return; when He suffered, He did not threaten, but committed Himself to Him who judges righteously; who Himself bore our sins in His own body on the tree, that we, having died to sins, might live for righteousness— by whose stripes you were healed. For you were like sheep going astray, but have now returned to the Shepherd and Overseer of your souls. (1 Peter 2:18-25)*

In his letters to the Jesus believers at Ephesus and Colosse, the apostle Paul addresses the relationship between slaves and masters (Ephesians 6:5-9; Colossians 3:22-4:1), and between husbands and wives (Ephesians 5:22-33; Colossians 3:18-19). Likewise, Peter deals with those same issues here in his letter to scattered believers. In the previous section, he called for believers to honor *all* people. This is how we experience the true freedom we have in Jesus the Messiah, by loving God and serving others. He also discussed the believer's relationship to governing authorities. Now he turns to the issue of slavery.

Slavery was a reality of Roman culture, but Peter voices neither approval nor disapproval of it. Instead, he undermines it. The kingdom of heaven is like leaven, Jesus said (Matthew 13:33), and that is how Peter appears to approach the matter of slavery. Writing to household servants, the class of slaves most likely to have access to this letter, he says, "Servants, submit to your masters with all due respect." Not only to those masters who are good and gentle but even to those who are harsh, and especially when treated unjustly.

It is commendable—praiseworthy, thankworthy, finds favor—if one puts up with being wrongfully penalized or is persecuted because of their faith in King Jesus the Messiah. This same faith, it turns out, is what would also enable them to endure unjust treatment. Of course, nobody gets praise for submitting to penalties that are deserved. But when one patiently endures punishment they have received, although they do not deserve it but have actually been "doing good" (there's that Greek word *agathapoieo* again, the giving of self that blesses others), that is the kind of response that finds favor with God. It may also win respect with masters and cause them to think more favorably about faith in Jesus. As Paul's letter to Philemon shows concerning the runaway slave, Onesimus, a master who belongs to Jesus can no longer think the same way about slavery, especially when the slave is his brother in the Lord. The entire institution must eventually yield to the love of God.

Peter then gives the supreme example for suffering while doing good, and how that brings about redemption. He draws from Isaiah 53, the prophet's portrayal of Messiah as the "Suffering Servant." Peter had witnessed firsthand how this was fulfilled in the Lord Jesus, who was persecuted and punished by men even though He was without sin or deceit. Yet, though shamefully abused, He did not respond in kind or threaten any vengeance. Rather, His words from the cross were, "Father, forgive them, for they do not know what they do" (Luke 23:34). Consider what the suffering of Jesus has done for us.

- He bore our sins in our place. In Him, we are now dead to sin and have the ability to do what is right before God.
- He took the stripes, the scourging we rightfully deserved, and we are now healed.
- We once were like sheep gone astray; now we are restored to the Shepherd and Guardian of our souls.

In a similar way, submitting humbly to those who have authority over us and doing good may cause them to turn to God through faith in Jesus the Messiah.

Focus Questions

1. In what ways can suffering for doing good undermine evil institutions?

2. What are the qualities or characteristics necessary to be able to do this?

3. Where do these qualities come from and how are they developed in us?

Transforming Marriages with True Freedom

Wives, likewise, be submissive to your own husbands, that even if some do not obey the word, they, without a word, may be won by the conduct of their wives, when they observe your chaste conduct accompanied by fear. Do not let your adornment be merely outward—arranging the hair, wearing gold, or putting on fine apparel—rather let it be the hidden person of the heart, with the incorruptible beauty of a gentle and quiet spirit, which is very precious in the sight of God. For in this manner, in former times, the holy women who trusted in God also adorned themselves, being submissive to their own husbands, as Sarah obeyed Abraham, calling him lord, whose daughters you are if you do good and are not afraid with any terror. (1 Peter 3:1-6)

Peter writes about the true freedom we now have because we belong to God through Jesus the Messiah. This liberty is not a thinly veiled license to live according to the lusts of the world. Rather, it is the freedom to love, give and serve, just as God revealed Himself in the example of Messiah.

All this is summed up for Peter in the words "be submissive." The Greek word is *hypotasso*, made up of two words: *hypo*, "under," and *tasso*, which has to do with order or arrangement. Literally, it means to subordinate. Peter began an earlier section with "Submit yourselves to every ordinance of man" (1 Peter 2:13). French theologian Ceslas Spicq thinks a better translation of the unusual Greek expression behind it is, "Submit to every human creature" (*Theological Lexicon of the New Testament*, p. 425 n. 9). This idea is reinforced a few verses later when Peter says, "Honor *all* people." What does it mean, in practical terms, to submit? Spicq offers this:

> It means first of all accepting the exact place God has assigned, keeping to one's rank in this or that society, accepting a dependent status, especially toward God (Jas 4:7), like children who are submissive to a father's discipline (Heb 12:9), after the fashion of the child Jesus. This religious subjection is made up of an obedient spirit, humaneness of heart, respect and willingness to serve. To submit is to accept directives that are given, to honor conditions that are imposed, to please one's superior (Titus 2:9) or honor him by the homage that is obedience (cf. Eph 6:1), to repudiate egotism and aloofness. It is to spontaneously position oneself as a servant towards one's neighbor in the hierarchy of love. (*Ibid.*, pp. 425-6).

Peter showed how this works in relation to governing authorities and how it can be redemptive for those trapped in slavery (which ensnares masters as well as slaves) in a way that actually undermines that institution. Now he speaks of how to live it out in the marriage relationship.

The bulk of his instruction in this present passage is for wives. Wives in the surrounding cultures did not enjoy equal status or honor with their husbands but were considered inferior, so they were the ones more likely to be treated unjustly. More specifically, Peter addresses those wives whose husbands were not believers. The prevailing religious culture would have simply expected them to worship the gods of their husbands. But Peter shows Christian wives how to approach this in a different and effective way: "Be submissive—spontaneously position yourselves as servants, in the hierarchy of love—to your own husbands." This does not mean giving up one bit of what the wives believe nor does it mean doing evil or committing injustice. Rather, the conduct of their lives should be pure, modest and innocent, with reverence toward God and respect toward their husbands. Even though these husbands may not be receptive to the word of the gospel in preaching or teaching, they might still be favorably influenced by the way they see it lived out in their wives and be won to faith in the Messiah.

It was fashionable, then as now, for women to adorn themselves in fine clothes, fancy hair and expensive jewelry. But for Christian wives, the emphasis should be on "the hidden person of the heart, with the incorruptible beauty of a gentle and quiet spirit." This pleases God and can transform one's marriage. Peter again uses the Greek word *aphthartos*, "incorruptible." He has already used it twice: In 1 Peter 1:4, he used it to describe the inheritance God has for us. In 1 Peter 1:23, he referred to the new life we have in Jesus through the incorruptible seed of the Word of God. Born of incorruptible seed for an incorruptible inheritance, we have an incorruptible beauty at work in us—a gentle and peaceful spirit. It is the fruit of the Holy Spirit (Galatians 5:22-23) and we must let Him bring forth that fruit in our lives. Sarah serves as an example here, who showed proper respect for Abraham but was not intimidated or afraid of him.

So far, Peter's comments have been for those wives whose husbands are not believers, so their husbands might come to share faith in the Messiah with them. Next, Peter has a word for husbands who are believers.

> *Husbands, likewise, dwell with them with understanding, giving honor to the wife, as to the weaker vessel, and as being heirs together of the grace of life, that your prayers may not be hindered.* (1 Peter 3:7)

Peter's instruction to husbands ran counter to the prevailing culture:

- *Husbands, likewise.* Husbands also are to be submissive to every human creature—including their wives.
- *Dwell with them with understanding.* The Greek word for "dwell with" is *synoikeo*, made up of two words: *syn*, "together," and oikeo, to occupy a house. It speaks of a domestic relationship. In the case of husband and wife, the husband is to have understanding for his wife in every aspect of their relationship.
- *Giving honor to the wife.* She is to be honored, just as he is. The Greek word for "honor" has a substantive value and, in this case, would include the husband properly providing for and taking caring of his wife.
- *As to the weaker vessel.* This does not refer to spiritual, moral or intellectual weakness but, rather, to physical weakness. A vessel is a container, just as the body may be thought of as a container for the soul.
- *And as being heirs together of the grace of life.* The Greek term for "heirs" here refers to *co-heirs* or *joint-heirs*. There is no inequality here; husbands and wives share equally in the inheritance of new life in Jesus. The husband is not spiritually superior to his wife; they are both the same before God. "There is neither Jew nor Greek, there is neither slave nor free, there is neither male nor female; for you are all one in Christ Jesus" (Galatians 3:28).

☞ *That your prayers may not be hindered.* Paul said that faith works through love (Galatians 5:6). If we are not walking in love towards our mates, it can hinder our faith and, consequently, our prayers.

As believers in Jesus, true freedom in marriage is found in mutual submission. It's not about who's the boss but who's the servant. We are each to love, give to and serve one another, not as scorekeepers or accountants, but generously and freely. It is because God so loved the world and Jesus came to give His life for us, that we are able to love one another in this way, bearing the fruit of the Spirit. It is how marriages become strong, and powerful in prayer and faith.

Focus Questions

1. According to Spicq, to submit is to "position oneself as a servant towards one's neighbor in the hierarchy of love." What would this look like in the marriage relationship?

2. Is there a difference between wives submitting to their husbands and husbands honoring their wives? Or between what Paul says in Ephesians 5:22, "Wives, submit to your husbands" and in Ephesians 5:25, "Husbands, love your wives"?

3. If a husband does not properly honor his wife, why or how would that hinder his prayer?

A Life of Blessing

Finally, all of you be of one mind, having compassion for one another; love as brothers, be tenderhearted, be courteous; not returning evil for evil or reviling for reviling, but on the contrary blessing, knowing that you were called to this, that you may inherit a blessing. For "He who would love life and see good days, let him refrain his tongue from evil, and his lips from speaking deceit. Let him turn away from evil and do good; let him seek peace and pursue it. For the eyes of the LORD are on the righteous, and His ears are open to their prayers; but the face of the LORD is against those who do evil." (1 Peter 3:8-12)

Peter has been dealing with how these new believers in Jesus, though they be treated as outcasts, are to treat the unbelieving world around them, as well as how they are to live with each other. This includes their obligations toward governing authorities, how slaves are to respond to their masters (even harsh masters) and how believing wives are to behave toward their unbelieving husbands. Now he brings these words for *all* believers, whatever their circumstances. The Greek tense for all of these indicate continuous action, not one-time deeds but a way of life.

- *Be of one mind.* Greek, *homophron*, of the "same mind." Living in harmony, with no divisions, having the same mind and the same purpose (Romans 15:6; 1 Corinthians 1:10; Philippians 1:27). Paul tells us, "Let this mind be in you which as also in Christ Jesus" (Philippians 2:5-8).
- *Having compassion for one another.* The Greek word is *sympatheis* and is made up of two parts: *sym* means "together;" *pathos* is the

experience of passion or suffering. This is where we get our word "sympathy." It is an openness to one another that moves one to act on behalf of another, especially in a time of need or distress.

- *Love as brothers.* Greek, *philadelphoi* (the name of Philadelphia, called "the city of brotherly love" comes from this word). We are to live together as loving brother and sisters, recognizing that we belong together in the same family, with the God and Father of Jesus the Messiah as our own Father.
- *Be tenderhearted.* The Greek word used here, *eusplagchnos*, speaks of a depth of feeling, kindness and mercy towards another, even as that of a mother for her child.
- *Be courteous.* Greek, *philophron*. Friendly-minded toward all, with the humility of love.

Peter is well aware that these believers are being treated unjustly, persecuted because of their faith, and that this will continue. But they are not to respond in kind, trading insults or retaliating with curses. Instead, they are to respond with blessing. This echoes the teaching of Jesus in the Sermon on the Mount:

> *But I say to you, love your enemies, bless those who curse you, do good to those who hate you, and pray for those who spitefully use you and persecute you, that you may be sons of your Father in heaven. (Matthew 5:44-45)*

God has called us to inherit a blessing and to live it out in the world, even when people are evil toward us. "Do not be overcome by evil, but overcome evil with good," Paul says (Romans 12:21). When we pay back evil for evil, we have been overcome by it, but when we pay back evil with blessing instead of cursing, we overcome it. It is, of course, a matter that requires faith: "This is the victory that has overcome the world—our faith" (1 John 5:4). We need to trust that God will sort things out properly and set everything right.

Peter then quotes from Psalm 34:12-16 (he alluded to Psalm 34:8 earlier, in 1 Peter 2:3, about tasting the goodness of the Lord). It is a song of thanksgiving David wrote about a time when he was living in exile among the Philistines and God answered his prayers for deliverance. It supports what Peter has been saying throughout this section: Those who want to enjoy a good life should refrain from speaking evil, but do good and diligently pursue peace. God looks with favor on those who do what is right, and He will answer their prayers. But let God deal with those who do evil and speak curses. This is how we live a life of blessing—blessing others and being blessed by God.

Focus Questions

1. What is the depth of love believers are to have for one another and what are its limits?

2. What are some practical demonstrations of this love?

3. How do the elements of mind, emotion and will work together in this? In what way is love a thought, a feeling, a choice?

A Ready Heart and a Gentle Response

And who is he who will harm you if you become followers of what is good? But even if you should suffer for righteousness' sake, you are blessed. "And do not be afraid of their threats, nor be troubled." But sanctify the Lord God in your hearts, and always be ready to give a defense to everyone who asks you a reason for the hope that is in you, with meekness and fear; having a good conscience, that when they defame you as evildoers, those who revile your good conduct in Christ may be ashamed. For it is better, if it is the will of God, to suffer for doing good than for doing evil. (1 Peter 3:13-17)

In the previous section, Peter spoke about loving one another and doing good to all, even to those who do us evil. If we return evil for evil, we become part of the problem. God knows how to reward those who do good and deal with those who do evil, so we can leave it in His hands.

Peter now asks a rhetorical question: "And who is he who will harm you if you become followers of what is good?" The word "and" shows that he is continuing the discussion he introduced in verses 8-12. People naturally tend to respond in kind, good for good, evil for evil. When we repay evil for evil, we only escalate the situation and increase the likelihood of coming to harm. If one suffers for doing evil, justice has been done; but if one suffers for doing good, the justice of God will set things right. If we return good for evil and blessing for cursing, we break the old cycle and establish a new one.

When we respond with good, it becomes harder for those who formerly did us evil to continue doing that. Harder, but not impossible. Though most people respond well to kindness and respect, there are still those who are bent on evil toward those they fear or with whom they disagree. Even so, we will still come out all right because we are blessed by God. Once again, Peter echoes Jesus' teaching on the mount:

> *Blessed are those who are persecuted for righteousness' sake, for theirs is the kingdom of heaven. Blessed are you when they revile and persecute you, and say all kinds of evil against you falsely for My sake. Rejoice and be exceedingly glad, for great is your reward in heaven, for so they persecuted the prophets who were before you. (Matthew 5:11-12)*

This puts us in very good company. Who, then, can harm us?

> *What then shall we say to these things? If God is for us, who can be against us? He who did not spare His own Son, but delivered Him up for us all, how shall He not with Him also freely give us all things? Who shall bring a charge against God's elect? It is God who justifies. Who is he who condemns? It is Christ who died, and furthermore is also risen, who is even at the right hand of God, who also makes intercession for us. Who shall separate us from the love of Christ? Shall tribulation, or distress, or persecution, or famine, or nakedness, or peril, or sword? ... Yet in all these things we are more than conquerors through Him who loved us. For I am persuaded that neither death nor life, nor angels nor principalities nor powers, nor things present nor things to come, nor height nor depth, nor any other created thing, shall be able to separate us from the love of God which is in Christ Jesus our Lord. (Romans 8:31-39)*

Therefore, do not be afraid, Peter says. He has Isaiah 8:12-14 in mind:

> *Do not say, "A conspiracy,"*
> *Concerning all that this people call a conspiracy,*
> *Nor be afraid of their threats, nor be troubled.*
> *The LORD of hosts, Him you shall hallow;*
> *Let Him be your fear,*
> *And let Him be your dread.*
> *He will be as a sanctuary,*
> *But a stone of stumbling and a rock of offense.*

He quoted verse 14 earlier, in 1 Peter 2:8, concerning the cornerstone that became a stone of stumbling and a rock of offense for those refused to believe. Now he draws from verse 12, "Do not be afraid of their threats, nor be troubled." And he makes allusion to verses 13 and 14, about *hallowing* the Lord and taking Him as a *sanctuary*: "But *sanctify* the Lord God in your hearts." The Greek tense of the verb here is aorist, which speaks of a completed action. In other words, Peter is telling us to settle the issue in a decisive way. The *HSCB* translates it as "But set apart the Messiah as Lord," reflecting the earliest copies of Peter's letter. Paul said,

> *If you confess with your mouth the Lord Jesus and believe in your heart that God has raised Him from the dead, you will be saved. For with the heart one believes unto righteousness, and with the mouth confession is made unto salvation. For the Scripture says, "Whoever believes on Him will not be put to shame." (Romans 10:9-11)*

When we confess Jesus as Lord and take our refuge in Him, we do not need to back down or fear anything man might do. This frees us to give a "defense" when people ask us about the hope we have, the joyful expectation of faith that is in us. The Greek word for "defense," *apologia*, refers to a reasoned statement in response to charges or questioning, whether in a court of law or informal conversation.

With our faith in God, we can present our case with gentleness and respect, keeping a clear conscience. Then we will not be put to shame, even when we are called evildoers; our good conduct will prove otherwise, and perhaps cause our accusers to back down.

Focus Questions

1. How is one blessed who suffers for righteousness' sake?

2. What does it means to sanctify the Lord God in our hearts? How do we do that?

3. What is the nature of the defense we make? In what way does it make appeal to the reasoning of the head, the heart, the will?

Suffering Messiah, Reigning King

For Christ also suffered once for sins, the just for the unjust, that He might bring us to God, being put to death in the flesh but made alive by the Spirit, by whom also He went and preached to the spirits in prison, who formerly were disobedient, when once the Divine longsuffering waited in the days of Noah, while the ark was being prepared, in which a few, that is, eight souls, were saved through water. There is also an antitype which now saves us—baptism (not the removal of the filth of the flesh, but the answer of a good conscience toward God), through the resurrection of Jesus Christ, who has gone into heaven and is at the right hand of God, angels and authorities and powers having been made subject to Him. (1 Peter 3:18-22)

Once again, Peter draws on the example of Jesus the Messiah to demonstrate his point that it is better to suffer for doing good than for doing evil. Jesus was just, yet He suffered for the sins of the unjust. He did that for a good purpose—that He might bring us to God!

Jesus was put to death in the flesh, His body nailed to a cross until He died. But He was made alive by the Spirit of God, resurrected in a spiritual body. Not spiritual as opposed to physical. It is still a body after all, but one empowered by the Holy Spirit. Paul describes this in 1 Corinthians 15, as he relates how the bodily resurrection of Jesus from the dead is the guarantee of resurrection for those who believe in Him: The same body that is sown in corruption is raised up incorruptible. The same body that is sown in dishonor is raised up in glory. The same body that is sown in weakness is raised up in power. The same body that is sown in mortality is raised up in immortality. The same body that is sown as a natural body is raised up as a spiritual body, empowered by the Holy Spirit.

It is by the Holy Spirit, whose power raised Him from the dead, that Jesus went and "preached" to the "spirits in prison." The word for "preached" refers to an authoritative proclamation, which can mean the announcement of good news or of triumph and judgment. Whether triumph and judgment is good news depends, of course, on which side of it you are on.

Who are these "spirits in prison" to whom Jesus makes proclamation? This is a difficult passage, but Peter does give us some important clues:

- They were those from an earlier time who had been disobedient.
- They were from the time of Noah.
- They were from a time when God was patiently waiting.

Some commentators think they are the spirits of men who did not believe God and live obediently before Him. In this view, the proclamation Jesus made to them was actually done through the preaching of Noah, by the Spirit, in that earlier time.

Others commentators think Peter is drawing on a common Jewish belief of the Second Temple era concerning the identity of the "sons of God" in Genesis 6, who took wives from among the "daughters of men." They were thought to have been fallen angels. Flavius Josephus, Jewish historian from the first century AD, held this view. The book of 1 Enoch, which is not part of the Bible but written in the first century BC, describes them as fallen angels who were now in prison, and tells of judgment being proclaimed on them. This apocryphal book was known to the early Church and was well regarded by it; the New Testament letter of Jude refers to it.

These "spirits" were from the days of Noah. God was waiting out a certain period of time—"Divine longsuffering," Peter calls it. God said, "My Spirit shall not strive with man forever, for he is indeed flesh; yet his days shall be one hundred and twenty years" (Genesis 6:3). He was not establishing the length of a man's life at 120 years; He was giving all men only 120 more years before He brought judgment, because He saw that "the wickedness of man was great in the earth, and that every intent of the thoughts of his heart was only evil continually" (v. 5). Then we are introduced to Noah with the words, "But Noah found grace in the eyes of the LORD" (v. 8).

Peter nests the example of Noah right in the middle of talking about Jesus' suffering. Think of the abuse Noah must have endured for the sake of faith and living rightly before God. Yet, even though he suffered, Noah and his family were the only ones delivered from destruction. Then Peter uses the figure of salvation through water as a type for baptism that saves us today. However, he carefully notes that baptism does not put away the "filth of the flesh," the sins that are committed in the body. Rather, it is the "answer of a good conscience toward God." The Greek word for "answer" speaks of a pledge, a commitment, a declaration.

In the previous section, Peter spoke about giving an answer to those who persecute us about the reason for our hope, with a ready heart, a gentle response and a "good conscience," because our faith is in God. Now he returns to the matter of a good conscience. It is the obedience of faith, corresponding to the faithful obedience of Noah and in contrast to the disobedience of the "spirits in prison." In the context of baptism, the "answer of a good conscience" would refer to the confession of faith given in response to questions that were asked, answered in good conscience as a true reflection of faith.

Baptism is a sign of faith in Jesus the Messiah, for it is through His resurrection, Peter tells us, that we are saved. Further, Jesus has now "gone into heaven and is at the right hand of God, angels and authorities and powers having been made subject to Him." Though He suffered for doing good, He has not only brought about salvation for all who believe in Him, but now reigns as Lord over all, and every offending angel, authority and power are subject to Him. Just as the world in Noah's day faced the judgment of God in the flood, while only Noah and his family were saved, and just as the disobedient "spirits in prison" were judged by the cross and resurrection of Jesus from the dead by the Spirit of God, so there is coming a day in which everyone who persecutes believers will have to face the judgment of King Jesus.

Focus Questions

1. What is the significance of baptism in the context of this passage?

2. How might this relate to the idea of "giving a defense" from the previous section?

3. What does it mean for you that Jesus is at the right hand of the Father and that every angel, power and authority is now subject to Him?

Armed with the Attitude of Jesus

Therefore, since Christ suffered for us in the flesh, arm yourselves also with the same mind, for he who has suffered in the flesh has ceased from sin, that he no longer should live the rest of his time in the flesh for the lusts of men, but for the will of God. For we have spent enough of our past lifetime in doing the will of the Gentiles—when we walked in lewdness, lusts, drunkenness, revelries, drinking parties, and abominable idolatries. In regard to these, they think it strange that you do not run with them in the same flood of dissipation, speaking evil of you. They will give an account to Him who is ready to judge the living and the dead. For this reason the gospel was preached also to those who are dead, that they might be judged according to men in the flesh, but live according to God in the spirit. (1 Peter 4:1-6)

Jesus the Messiah was put to death in the flesh for our sake, because of our sin. He conquered death through resurrection from the dead by the Holy Spirit and has been exalted by God to the right hand of the Father, where He rules and reigns over all. The dominion of sin has been broken; the dominion of Messiah has begun.

Because Jesus has suffered the cross in our place, He has won for us our freedom. Just as He has been raised from the dead, we also are given new life in Him. Once we were spiritually dead and under the sentence of physical death, but no more. That is what the sign of baptism is about in the previous section. Paul put it very similarly:

> *Therefore we were buried with Him through baptism into death, that just as Christ was raised from the dead by the glory of the Father, even so we also should walk in newness of life. For if we have been united together in the likeness of His death, certainly we also shall be in the likeness of His resurrection, knowing this, that our old man was crucified with Him, that the body of sin might be done away with, that we should no longer be slaves of sin. For he who has died has been freed from sin. (Romans 6:4-7)*

We are to "arm" ourselves with the same "mind" Jesus showed. There is a militancy in the word "arm." It does not speak of passivity but of preparedness, even aggressiveness. The Greek word used for "mind" here speaks of intent, resolve, attitude. We are to prepare ourselves with the same attitude that Jesus had: He suffered under our sin at the cross, but now He is done with it—He has dominion over it! As Paul put it, "He who has died has been freed from sin." That is to be our attitude: We are freed from sin. "He who has suffered in the flesh has ceased from sin, that he no longer should live the rest of his time in the flesh for the lusts of men, but for the will of God," Peter says. He and Paul track very closely on this.

> *Likewise you also, reckon yourselves to be dead indeed to sin, but alive to God in Christ Jesus our Lord. Therefore do not let sin reign in your mortal body, that you should obey it in its lusts. And do not present your members as instruments of unrighteousness to sin, but present yourselves to God as being alive from the dead, and your members as instruments of righteousness to God. For sin shall not have dominion over you. (Romans 6:11-14)*

This is the attitude we are to arm ourselves with: We are to reckon ourselves dead to sin but alive to God in King Jesus the Messiah. No longer living according to the lusts of the flesh, the former way of life we used to know before we were set free. Peter gives a brief description here. There is no need to run down the list. They are all pretty bad. Worse than bad. Paul gives a similar list in Galatians 5:19-21 under the name "works of the flesh." They are all things that tear down families, destroy communities and break apart the world. There is no life at all to them; they stink of death. The world has seen more than enough of them. It is time for true life and freedom to be revealed, the life and freedom that are found in King Jesus and empowered by the Holy Spirit. Opposite the "works of the flesh," Paul details the "fruit of the Spirit" in Galatians 5:22-23: Love, joy, peace, longsuffering, kindness, goodness, faithfulness, gentleness, self-control.

Now, ironically, those who are still caught in the "works of the flesh" find this threatening. Old friends with whom we once carried on in the ways of the world may be confused that we no longer behave in those old ways. In Peter's day, those who believed in Jesus were being persecuted because of their faith and their way of life. But those who persist in their unbelief and persecute those who do believe will have to give account to King Jesus when He comes to set things right among the living and the dead. Even those who are now physically dead, if they have believed the good news about Him, will be made alive again by the Spirit of God, and those who have been martyred in the flesh will be vindicated in the Spirit, just as Jesus was.

Focus Questions

1. What is the mind of Jesus we are to arm ourselves with?

2. Why does this need to become *our* mindset, too?

3. What needs to change in your own thinking in order to do this?

The End is Here?

But the end of all things is at hand. (1 Peter 4:7)

At the end of chapter 3, Peter referred to the events and circumstances of Genesis 6, namely, the disobedient spirits, the flood and the ark. It seems that he still has that in mind when he says, "The end of all things is at hand," because it echoes God's words to Noah in Genesis 6:13, "The end of all flesh has come before Me, for the earth is filled with violence through them; and behold, I will destroy them with the earth." There, it meant that the time had come to put an end to all the violence and corruption that was rife in Noah's day. The world was no less corrupt in Peter's day. Was he expecting a judgment that never came? Was he mistaken about the end of all things being at hand?

In the New Testament, to say that something is "at hand" means that it is very near, within reach, and often, that it has actually arrived and is now present. Jesus came preaching that the kingdom of God was "at hand" (Matthew 4:17) and sent His disciples out to announce the same thing (Matthew 10:7). It was not far off, it was not *almost* here; it was *now present*. When asked by the Pharisees when the kingdom would come, Jesus answered, "The kingdom of God is among you" (Luke 17:21).

The kingdom of God has come into the world and has been expanding ever since. Jesus said, "From the days of John the Baptist until now, the kingdom of heaven has been forcefully advancing, and forceful men lay hold of it" (Matthew 11:12 *NIV*). Before Jesus ascended to the throne of heaven, the disciples asked if He was restoring the kingdom to Israel at that time. He neither affirmed nor denied. They were asking about times and seasons, the *when* of the kingdom, but Jesus answered in regard to the *how*: "You will receive power when the Holy Spirit has come upon you, and you will be My witnesses in Jerusalem, in all Judea and Samaria, and to the ends of the earth" (Acts 1:8). It is through the power of the Holy Spirit and the apostolic witness that all the nations of the earth are discipled and baptized and instructed in everything Jesus taught the first disciples (Matthew 28:19-20). For all authority in heaven and on earth has now been given to Him (Matthew 28:18). In other words, the kingdom of God has come into the world and King Jesus now reigns over all.

But what is the *end*? In Matthew 24, after Jesus spoke to Peter and the other disciples about the coming desolation of the temple in Jerusalem, they asked, "When will these things be? And what will be the sign of Your coming, and of the end of the age (v. 3). Jesus answered in terms of the destruction of Jerusalem, saying that it would happen in their generation (vv. 4-34). This was fulfilled in August of AD 70, with the destruction of Jerusalem and the temple, only a few years after Peter wrote this letter. For the Jews, this was the end of the age. (I deal more extensively with all this in *The Kingdom of Heaven on Earth: Keys to the Kingdom of God in the Gospel of Matthew*.)

The coming of God's kingdom into the world is the end of all other kingdoms. It must increase, as the nations believe the good news of the gospel and yield to King Jesus. The kingdom of darkness must give way to the kingdom of light. As the apostle John said, "The darkness is passing away and the true light is already shining" (1 John 2:8). The commission Jesus gave the disciples in Matthew 28 will not fail but succeed, for it comes with all the authority that was given to Jesus in heaven and on earth.

Peter was not mistaken. With the beginning of God's kingdom age, the end of all things is indeed at hand—now here—as the old age passes away.

Focus Questions

1. What are the things that are coming to end?

2. Why are they coming to an end?

3. What is the new thing that is coming into the world?

Manifesting the Glory and Dominion of Jesus

But the end of all things is at hand; therefore be serious and watchful in your prayers. And above all things have fervent love for one another, for "love will cover a multitude of sins." Be hospitable to one another without grumbling. As each one has received a gift, minister it to one another, as good stewards of the manifold grace of God. If anyone speaks, let him speak as the oracles of God. If anyone ministers, let him do it as with the ability which God supplies, that in all things God may be glorified through Jesus Christ, to whom belong the glory and the dominion forever and ever. Amen. (1 Peter 4:7-11)

The age of God's kingdom has come into the world, bringing to a close this "present evil age," as Paul calls it (Galatians 1:4). "The darkness is passing away and the true light is already shining," is how John put it (1 John 2:8). The kingdom has come but it has not yet arrived in all its fullness. We are living in the in-between time, and that requires certain things of us:

- ≈ Self-control and a clear head, so we can attend to the work of effective prayer.
- ≈ Devoted, focused love for one another. There is no room for carrying grudges and holding on to unforgiveness.
- ≈ Cheerful hospitality, welcoming each other with an open heart, an open house, an open or generous hand.

Every believer in Jesus the Messiah has received a *charisma*, a grace-gift from God. These are given for the benefit of all so that we may minister the multi-faceted grace of God to each other. Paul calls these *spirituals* and *manifestations* of the Holy Spirit, and goes into much detail about how they operate (1 Corinthians 12-14). Peter keeps it simple.

- Paul spoke of revelatory gifts (word of knowledge, word of wisdom and discerning of spirits) and spent much time on the operation of the gifts of divine speech (prophecy, tongues and interpretation of tongues). For Peter, those with speaking gifts should be careful to give God's words, not their own.
- Paul talked about manifestations of power (faith, gifts of healings and workings of miracles), and in Romans 12:6-8, mentioned gifts of service (serving, giving, leading, showing mercy). For Peter, in addition to gifts of speaking, there are gifts of doing, or ministering, or serving. Those who serve are to do so, not depending on their own natural ability, but with the ability that God supplies.

The function of all these gifts is to serve one another and build each other up, but the purpose is that God may be glorified in Jesus the Messiah, because it is His dominion that makes it possible for us to live and serve in these ways. The ability to do these things comes from God. They manifest the reality of His kingdom and demonstrate that the age of darkness is passing away and the true light of God's kingdom is already shining.

Focus Questions

1. What is required of us in this time of transition from the end of this "present evil age" to the kingdom of God coming into the world?

2. How do these things demonstrate the coming of God's kingdom into the world?

3. How does the ability of God operate in us and how do we operate in it?

An Unexpected Cause for Rejoicing

Beloved, do not think it strange concerning the fiery trial which is to try you, as though some strange thing happened to you; but rejoice to the extent that you partake of Christ's sufferings, that when His glory is revealed, you may also be glad with exceeding joy. If you are reproached for the name of Christ, blessed are you, for the Spirit of glory and of God rests upon you. On their part He is blasphemed, but on your part He is glorified. But let none of you suffer as a murderer, a thief, an evildoer, or as a busybody in other people's matters. Yet if anyone suffers as a Christian, let him not be ashamed, but let him glorify God in this matter. (1 Peter 4:12-16)

"Do not think it strange," Peter says to those being persecuted for their faith in Jesus, "as though some strange thing happened to you." It probably did seem strange to them, and to us, too. Are not believers in Jesus a new kind of people—a chosen generation, a royal priesthood, a holy nation, God's own special people (1 Peter 2:9)? Does not King Jesus the Messiah, in whom we believe, now rule and reign at the right hand of God the Father (1 Peter 3:22)? And does not all glory and dominion belong to Him now and forever (1 Peter

4:11)? How is it, then, that believers must endure such harsh treatment from the world?

"Fiery trials" will come. Literally, the Greek word refers to smelting, the process of extracting useful metals from useless ore by the application of extreme heat. It is like the refining process Peter referred to in 1 Peter 1:7, where the end result is a faith "more precious than gold." What he might have had in mind here, as difficult as it is to think about, were the Christian martyrs in Rome who were being burned alive as torches in Nero's gardens, giving a new and terrible reality to "fiery trial."

To "try" something means to test or prove it. The enemy tests us because he wants to see us fail and fall away from the faith; God allows it because He wants us to succeed and move forward in faith. The enemy wants us to suffer and be full of fear; God wants to reveal His glory in us and fill us with joy. The enemy intends for it to destroy us; God allows it to refine us. (It is important to understand that the real enemy here is not those who persecute but the evil one who motivates them.)

The outcome for us is assured—God will bring us through—so there is no reason for us to fear persecution. Indeed, Peter finds in it reason for "exceeding joy." This is the third time he has used the word *agalliao*, which signifies exuberant rejoicing (see 1 Peter 1:6-8). However, it is not in suffering itself that Peter rejoices, but in what it signifies, for both now and the future.

- It shows that when King Jesus returns at the end of the age and His glory is revealed, we shall share in it with Him. The apostle Paul, likewise, speaks of suffering and being glorified together with Jesus. "And if children, then heirs—heirs of God and joint heirs with Christ, if indeed we suffer with Him, that we may also be glorified together" (Romans 8:17). Suffering persecution for Jesus' sake is also a sign that we are heirs of God and joint heirs with Christ.

- It shows that the Spirit of glory and of God rests upon us. This is the Spirit of God, the Holy Spirit, who here is called the Spirit of Glory. The word "rests" means that He abides with us. He does not come and go, He stays with us. Notice the present tense; not *rested* or *will rest*, but the Spirit of Glory *rests* on us—just as He rested on Jesus. When we are reproached because of our faith in Jesus, it is actually the Holy Spirit who is being dishonored by those who persecute us, while He is honored by our faith and honors us with His presence. He is not just *with* us but *upon* us, which means that His presence becomes evident to us and to others.

There is no glory in suffering for being a murderer, a thief, an evildoer or a meddler. These are usually scorned by society, as they were in those days, and rightly so. For the Gentiles, however, believers in Jesus belonged in the same category and were called "Christians" as a term of derision. But what the world treats shamefully, Peter takes as honor: When you are reproached for the name of Christ and called "Christian," do not take that as a badge of disgrace but as an opportunity to give thanks to God.

This was not just theory for Peter. He lived it. When he and some of the other apostles were brought before the Sanhedrin and admonished for preaching Jesus, Peter answered, "We ought to obey God rather then men." On advice from Gamaliel that this movement would probably come to nothing, the council released Peter and the apostles. "So they departed from the presence of the council, rejoicing that they were counted worthy to suffer shame for His name. And daily in the temple, and in every house, they did not cease teaching and preaching Jesus as the Christ" (Acts 5:41-42).

Focus Questions

1. Many Jesus believers are being maimed and martyred in the world today, and many are experiencing persecution and rejection. Why might this seem to be a strange thing?

2. Why is it not a strange thing after all?

3. How does it lead to extreme joy, as it has for so many who have gone through intense persecution today?

Deliverance in Difficult Times

> *For the time has come for judgment to begin at the house of God; and if it begins with us first, what will be the end of those who do not obey the gospel of God? Now "If the righteous one is scarcely saved, where will the ungodly and the sinner appear?" Therefore let those who suffer according to the will of God commit their souls to Him in doing good, as to a faithful Creator.* (1 Peter 4:17-19)

Peter speaks of a judgment that is at hand. The Greek word for "time" here is *kairos*, not time as measured by clock or calendar but a pregnant and propitious moment of significant fulfillment. Notice, he does not say that the time for judgment *will come* but that it *has come*. This remains true today as countless believers are persecuted and martyred in the world because of their faith in Jesus the Messiah. This judgment begins at the "house of God." Peter is alluding to a couple of prophetic passages from the Old Testament (Jeremiah 25:15-9; Ezekiel 9:6) that speak of God's judgment on His disobedient people. However, he uses it quite differently here. Judgment begins at the house, or household, of God. "With us first," he says. Not the judgment of God on His disobedient people but the judgment exercised by the world on God's faithful ones. Those who believe the gospel of King Jesus the Messiah are being judged and persecuted by the world, but there is coming a time in which God Himself will judge those who *refuse* to believe (which is what the Greek word behind "disobey" means). The persecution believers may experience now cannot compare to the judgment that awaits those who do not obey the gospel, that is, those who willfully reject King Jesus.

Peter may also have had in mind the coming destruction of Jerusalem and the temple, which was foretold by Jesus in Matthew 24 and fulfilled in AD 70, just a few years after this letter. It was a time of great tribulation and bloodshed for the Jews, but those who believed in Jesus, having been warned by Him of this terrible holocaust, were for the most part able to escape desolation.

Peter quotes Proverbs 11:31, "If the righteous one is scarcely saved, where will the ungodly and the sinner appear?" This is not how it is rendered from the Hebrew text but from the Septuagint, an early Greek translation of the Hebrew, and speaks more directly to Peter's purpose. The use of "saved" here does not refer to eternal salvation of the soul but of deliverance in the time of trouble. The word "scarcely" means "with difficulty," and indeed that was the case for these believers. It was a very rough time for them. If it is difficult for persecuted believers, how much more difficult will it be for their persecutors when God comes and sets things right?

"Therefore," Peter says, as he introduces the response such a time of persecution calls for, "let those who suffer according to the will of God commit their souls *to Him* in doing good, as to a faithful Creator."

The will of God here is not what He *prescribed* but what He *permitted*. God *allows* persecutions to come on His people—indeed, Jesus promised us there would be persecutions (Mark 10:30)—but He does not *abandon* us to them. He is faithful and we can trust Him to see us through every trial and circumstance.

Notice in this verse that the words "to Him" are in italics. There is no textual basis for this, but translators supplied it in an attempt to help make the text more understandable. It leads us in the proper direction; we are to commit ourselves to God our creator. But leave out those italicized words and we discover how we are to do just that. We trust ourselves to Him by "doing good." Here again is that word *agathapoios*, which we saw in 1 Peter 2:15 and 20, the giving of self that blesses others.

God has created us—Paul says that those who are in the Messiah are a new creation (2 Corinthians 5:17)—and He will continue to take care of us no matter what. The way we commit ourselves to His faithful care is by continuing to do good to others, no matter what. That is how we live in the freedom we now have in Jesus. In this way, we commit ourselves to God as our faithful Creator.

Identifying God as Creator refers us, in turn, to creation itself and God's purpose for it. "Doing good," even under intense persecution, somehow brings fulfillment to Gods' purpose for creation. Paul said,

> *For I consider that the sufferings of this present time are not worthy to be compared with the glory which shall be revealed in us. For the earnest expectation of the creation eagerly waits for the revealing of the sons of God. For the creation was subjected to futility, not willingly, but because of Him who subjected it in hope; because the creation itself also will be delivered from the bondage of corruption into the glorious liberty of the children of God. (Romans 8:18-21)*

Focus Questions

1. What should be the attitude of the persecuted toward their persecutors?

2. Why does Peter turn again here to "doing good" (*agathapoios*), the giving of self for the sake of others?

3. How might "doing good" bring fulfillment to God's purpose for creation?

Wearing the Victor's Crown

> *So I exhort the elders among you, as a fellow elder and a witness of the sufferings of Christ, as well as a partaker in the glory that is going to be revealed: shepherd the flock of God that is among you, exercising oversight, not under compulsion, but willingly, as God would have you; not for shameful gain, but eagerly; not domineering over those in your charge, but being examples to the flock. And when the chief Shepherd appears, you will receive the unfading crown of glory. (1 Peter 5:1-4)*

Everything Peter has said up to this point has been for believers in general. Now he has a few words for the elders, leaders in the churches to whom the people would naturally look, especially in times of crisis. "Shepherd the flock of God," he tells them. This is the same charge Jesus gave to Peter in John 21:16, "Tend My sheep." It is the charge Paul gave to the elders at Ephesus: "Take heed to yourselves and to all the flock, among which the Holy Spirit has made you overseers, to shepherd the church of God which He purchased with His own blood" (Acts 20:28). It is the pastoral function—the Greek word for "shepherd" is the same word for "pastor."

The role of shepherds is simple, though not always easy even in the best of times. They see that the flock is fed, keep it from straying, and protect it from wolves, snares and other dangers. They "exercise oversight." The Greek word is *episkopeo*, which means to watch over, look after and care for the flock, being alert to danger or problems. The author of Hebrews, writing to Jesus believers who were under fire, uses this same term in a way that emphasizes its diligent nature: "Looking carefully [*episkopeo*] lest anyone fall short of the grace of God; lest any root of bitterness springing up cause trouble, and by this many become defiled; lest there be any fornicator or profane person like Esau, who for one morsel of food sold his birthright" (Hebrews 12:15-16).

To be a good shepherd and properly exercise oversight requires the motivation of a pure heart. Peter breaks this down by way of three contrasts:

- *Not under compulsion, but willingly.* No shepherd should feel pressured into this work but should be able to serve with a willing heart, for it can be a very difficult business, and a risky one in perilous times.
- *Not for shameful gain, but eagerly.* Elders who rule well are worthy of double honor (1 Timothy 5:17) and those who are taught in the Word should share with their teachers (Galatians 6:6), but this is not to be the motivation for elders and teachers. They are not to be lovers of money, as were some of the Pharisees (Luke 16:14). They are not to be eager for gain, calculating a return, but eager

to serve out of love and devotion. True shepherds lay down their lives for the sheep, but hirelings run away when trouble comes (John 10:11-13).

- *Not domineering, but being an example.* Shepherds are not to act like lords over an allotment, or masters over a possession. Their job is not to overcome, subjugate, subdue or force the flock into submission. Rather, they are to lead the flock God has entrusted to them by the example of their own faithful lives.

As shepherds, elders are accountable to the Chief Shepherd, and when He comes again, those who have served faithfully will receive the "unfading crown of glory." This is the victor's crown, the wreath given to those who have won their race. Paul spoke similarly as he came to the end of his own apostolic career: "I have fought the good fight, I have finished the race, I have kept the faith. Finally, there is laid up for me the crown of righteousness, which the Lord, the righteous Judge, will give to me on that Day, and not to me only but also to all who have loved His appearing" (1 Timothy 4:7-8). It is an unfading crown, like the incorruptible inheritance God has reserved for all who trust in Him (1 Peter 1:4).

Focus Questions

1. Why is the role of shepherd important?

2. Why are the qualities Peter outlines important to that role?

3. How does Jesus fulfill the role of shepherd?

Clothing Yourself with Greatness

Likewise you younger people, submit yourselves to your elders. Yes, all of you be submissive to one another, and be clothed with humility. (1 Peter 5:5)

Peter exhorted the elders of these scattered churches to "shepherd the flock of God," willingly and eagerly, leading not as lords but as examples. Next, he turns to those younger in the faith, who are under the spiritual care of these shepherds: "Likewise … submit yourselves to your elders." He directs them to respond to the elders in the same way he directs the elders to lead them: willingly, eagerly, following their example.

The word for "submit" is *hypotasso*, the same word Peter used numerous times in chapter 2, of obeying governing authorities and honoring all people, of servants obeying their masters, of wives serving their husbands—and by submitting to all, exercising the true freedom we have in King Jesus the Messiah. Remember Spicq's description regarding the meaning of this Greek word and what it means to submit: "to spontaneously position oneself as a servant towards one's neighbor in the hierarchy of love."

Now, he broadens his exhortation to include both elders and younger: "Yes, *all of you*, be submissive to one another." The elders are to be just as submissive to the younger as the younger are to be to the elders. Submission is never a question about who is the boss; it is always about who is the servant, for those who are greatest in the kingdom of God are those who serve (Matthew 20:25-28).

This is really quite a radical thing Peter is telling them, for he adds, "… and be clothed with humility." This is the heart of one who serves. The Greek word for "clothed" used here is *egkomboomai*;

from *komboo*, the word for "knot" or "buckle." It refers to tying on or fastening together garments such as aprons—the clothes of a servant. It is cast in the middle voice, which means we must clothe ourselves, taking upon ourselves the humble attitude of a servant.

Peter knew exactly what this looked like. On the night of the Last Supper, he saw the Lord Jesus do exactly that, how He "rose from supper and laid aside His garments, took a towel and girded Himself. After that, He poured water into a basin and began to wash the disciples' feet, and to wipe them with the towel with which He was girded" (John 13:4-5). At first, Peter did not understand and was embarrassed for Jesus to wash his feet. Jesus answered, "What I am doing you do not understand now, but you will know after this" (v. 7). When He finished washing all their feet, He sat down and said,

> *Do you know what I have done to you? You call Me Teacher and Lord, and you say well, for so I am. If I then, your Lord and Teacher, have washed your feet, you also ought to wash one another's feet. For I have given you an example, that you should do as I have done to you. Most assuredly, I say to you, a servant is not greater than his master; nor is he who is sent greater than he who sent him. If you know these things, blessed are you if you do them." (John 13:12-17)*

Jesus clothed Himself with servant humility from the beginning. I call it the "algebra of love": God is love (1 John 4:8), love gives and serves (John 3:16; Mark 10:45). Even now, Jesus makes intercession for us at the right hand of God (Romans 8:34). If He has become the servant of all, should not we, then, also serve each other? Paul said,

Let this mind be in you which was also in Christ Jesus, who, being in the form of God, did not consider it robbery to be equal with God, but made Himself of no reputation, taking the form of a bondservant, and coming in the likeness of men. And being found in appearance as a man, He humbled Himself and became obedient to the point of death, even the death of the cross. Therefore God also has highly exalted Him and given Him the name which is above every name. (Philippians 2:5-9)

It is in clothing ourselves with humility and serving one another that we clothe ourselves with greatness in the kingdom of God.

Focus Questions

1. What does the role of shepherd, from the previous section, look like in regard to submission?

2. What is the relationship between submission and humility?

3. What is the relationship between Jesus, submission and humility?

Under the Mighty Hand of God

Yes, all of you be submissive to one another, and be clothed with humility, for "God resists the proud, but gives grace to the humble." Therefore humble yourselves under the mighty hand of God, that He may exalt you in due time, casting all your care upon Him, for He cares for you. (1 Peter 5:5-7)

Peter teaches us that we are to be clothed with humility and serve one another. He quotes Proverbs 3:34 (from the Septuagint version, the Greek translation of the Hebrew text).

God "resists" the proud. The Greek word is *antitassomai*, from the same root as *hypotasso*, the word for "submit." The verb stem, *tasso*, means to arrange or set. The prefix *hypo* means to be under something. When we are submissive, we are arranged or set under whatever it is we are submitted to. The prefix *anti* means to be against. The word *antitassomai* is set in the middle voice, which means that God arranges Himself against the proud. The point is clear: If we are not willing to be submissive to one another, God will set Himself in opposition against us. On the other hand, if we will learn to serve each other with a spirit of humility, God will pour out His grace upon us. The grace of God is His favor, His willingness to release all the power and authority of heaven on our behalf. The contrast could not be sharper: God is ready to arrange Himself for us or against us, depending on our willingness to serve and submit to one another.

The answer, of course, is that we should allow ourselves to be humbled under the mighty hand of God. The Greek word for "humble yourselves," is actually in the passive voice, "allow yourselves to be humbled." Do not resist, but yield yourself to Him. Whenever the mighty hand of God is revealed, it is always for the benefit of His friends but against His foes. If we are humble and willing, the mighty hand of God is not against us but for us, and He is gracious to get us where we need to be. He will teach and empower us for His way of loving, giving and serving. Then when the "due time" (Greek, *kairos*, the poignant or proper moment) comes, He will exalt us, even as He exalted Jesus.

Loving and serving one another are all the more important in times of trouble or persecution, when it can be so easy for us to focus on our own needs to the neglect of each other. But Peter assures us that we are in good hands. When we allow God to teach us humility, we can "cast our cares" over onto Him, because He will take care of us. The Greek word for "cast" means to fling or toss, to hurl in a sudden motion. There are two different Greek words for "care" used here. The first one ("cast your *care*") refers to the distractions and anxieties of life that so often eat away at us, sapping our strength and destroying our peace of mind. These are the cares we are to quickly heave over onto Him—they are now His problem to deal with, and He knows very well how to handle them. The second word ("He *cares* for you") speaks of the interest or concern God has for us. He will take care of everything we need, freeing us to care for each other.

Focus Questions

1. What is the relationship between humility and exaltation?

2. What is the relationship between humility and casting our cares on God?

3. How does God's care for us free us to submit to and serve others?

Standing Firm Against the Adversary

Be sober, be vigilant; because your adversary the devil walks about like a roaring lion, seeking whom he may devour. Resist him, steadfast in the faith, knowing that the same sufferings are experienced by your brotherhood in the world. But may the God of all grace, who called us to His eternal glory by Christ Jesus, after you have suffered a while, perfect, establish, strengthen, and settle you. To Him be the glory and the dominion forever and ever. Amen. (1 Peter 5:8-11)

Peter identifies the real enemy for us. Not Rome, not the surrounding communities and cultures, not even Nero, but "your adversary *the devil*." He was well aware that this was a *spiritual* warfare, a very real one, but in the realm of the spirit. As Paul said, "We do not wrestle against flesh and blood, but against principalities, against powers, against the rulers of the darkness of this age, against spiritual hosts of wickedness in the heavenly places" (Ephesians 6:12). These are demonic entities that influence systems such as government, culture, education and economy against those who follow the way of King Jesus.

The Greek word for "adversary" is *antidikos*, made up of two words: *anti*, which means "against," and *dikos*, which speaks of what is right and just. Literally, it refers to an opponent in a lawsuit. The name *satan* means "adversary" and he is called the "accuser of the brethren" (Revelation 12:10). The Greek word for "devil," means "slanderer." He comes making accusation against us, slandering us before God, before others and even before ourselves. He seeks to turn the world against us and is the source behind all persecution.

The devil is like a roaring lion look for someone to destroy. Though speaking figuratively, Peter may also have had in mind the Christians at Rome who were literally being thrown to the lions. "Resist him," Peter says. The Greek word, *antihistemi*, means to take a stand against. When the devil comes against us with lies and persecutions, we are to stand against him by staying firm in the faith. Notice the definite article, "*the* faith." The focus is on the object of our faith, King Jesus the Messiah. The apostle James said: "Therefore submit to God. Resist the devil and he will flee from you" (James 4:7). First, we submit ourselves to God, taking our stand in Him. Then we will be well positioned to stand against the devil.

The attack of the adversary was not against these scattered churches alone, nor would they be alone in standing against him. There were many other believers also experiencing the same persecution—and faithfully resisting the devil. Again, Peter may have had in mind the tribulation believers faced at Rome. But they also had something much more powerful going for them, which Peter brings out by way of his closing benediction. The "God of all grace" would be with them, and the adversary is no match for that. God has called us to eternal glory by Jesus the Messiah. The relatively brief times of persecution—the word for "a while" actually means "a little"—do not compare to the rich and eternal inheritance we have in Him.

The grace of God is here to "perfect, establish, strengthen and settle" us. The word for "perfect" has a range of meaning, any of which would be encouraging for those facing difficult times: to prepare, repair, restore, equip, make whole. To "establish" means to stabilize, make firm or constant. "Strengthen" means to make strong in body or soul; here, with the strength that comes from God. "Be strong in the Lord and in the power of His might," Paul said (Ephesians 6:10). To "settle" means to set on a firm foundation.

Peter finishes with a doxology, a praise to the God of all grace for this eternal glory: "To Him be the glory and the dominion forever and ever. Amen." It is *His* glory and *His* dominion that will endure long after every persecution and difficulty has passed away.

Focus Questions

1. Peter and James both tell us to "resist the devil." How do we go about doing that?

2. How does knowing that other believers are going through the same thing help us resist the devil?

3. How does resisting the devil reveal the glory and dominion of King Jesus?

The Grace of God in Which We Stand

> *By Silvanus, our faithful brother as I consider him, I have written to you briefly, exhorting and testifying that this is the true grace of God in which you stand.*
>
> *She who is in Babylon, elect together with you, greets you; and so does Mark my son. Greet one another with a kiss of love.*
>
> *Peace to you all who are in Christ Jesus. Amen. (1 Peter 5:12-14)*

Peter ends his letter with a few personal notes, but even so, he is still bringing his message. Here is Silvanus, whose name is a variation on the name Silas. He is likely the same Silas who served and suffered with Paul (Acts 15-18) and emerged with strong faith. In Peter's mind, he has proven himself to be a faithful brother and, therefore, a worthy example of exactly what Peter was exhorting believers to do. Silvanus, or Silas, served as Peter's scribe or secretary for this letter, recording his message to the churches.

Here also is Mark. This is John Mark, who was Barnabas' nephew, or perhaps cousin (Colossians 4:10). He went out with Paul and Barnabas on a missionary journey (Acts 12:25) but soon turned back for home and for some reason did not continue on with them "to the work" (Acts 15:38). Because of that, when Barnabas wanted to bring Mark on another mission, Paul refused. The disagreement between Paul and Barnabas was so sharp over this that they split up, Barnabas taking Mark and Paul taking Silas (Acts 15:37-40). Paul eventually realized that Mark was a faithful brother after all (Colossians 4:10; 2 Timothy 4:11). Mark also became a very important part of Peter's ministry. Early Church history indicates that the Gospel According to Mark represents the preaching of Peter. Here, Peter calls him, "my son." He was martyred in the region of modern-day Libya, not very many years after Peter was crucified. For more on his remarkable story, see Thomas Oden's, *The Ancient Memory of Mark*.

"Babylon" may be a reference to Rome. As Babylon was a place of exile for Israel, Rome symbolized a place of exile for the Church. Or it might have been the Babylon that was in Egypt. Wherever it was, the "She" Peter speaks of is the church that was there, which was not separate from the other churches scattered throughout the provinces but one with them, chosen together with them by God.

Peter sums up why he has written this letter: to exhort and testify. The Greek word for "exhort" is *parakaleo*. Literally, it pictures one coming alongside and calling out to another. By usage it means to exhort or encourage. The churches to whom Peter wrote, scattered and rejected as they were, could certainly use encouragement as they faced continued harassment from unbelievers. His exhortations were also very practical, about the transformative power of love in serving others. He hits this a final lick with, "Greet one another with a kiss of love," once again bringing together the words "one another" and "love" (see 1 Peter 1:22).

Peter also "testified" to them and this was what they needed to hear the most. In difficult times, it can be very easy to waver or doubt: Is Jesus really God's promised Messiah who came to repair the world and rescue the people of God? Has the kingdom of God really come into the world and is Jesus really Lord over all? Peter's testimony is a resounding *Yes!*: "This is the true grace of God in which you stand." Yes! the resurrection of Jesus the Messiah from the dead gives us a living hope and an incorruptible inheritance. Yes! this inheritance is being preserved for us in heaven, kept by the power of God. And yes! it will be fully revealed on the earth in the "last time," God's great *kairos* moment when heaven and earth will be brought together into one, the will of God being done on earth exactly as it is in heaven.

This is the grace of God in which everyone who receives Jesus as Messiah and Lord now stands, the truth in which we live and abide. Because it is true, Peter is able to give this final benediction, "Peace to you all who are in Christ Jesus. Amen." Again, Peter would be thinking of the Hebrew *shalom*, the peace and wholeness that comes from God and belongs to all who belong to His Messiah King.

Focus Questions

1. Who are your own examples of keeping the faith when things get tough, and what do you learn from them?

2. How do Peter's exhortations and his own testimony show that this is indeed the true grace of God in which we stand?

3. How important is our love for each other in enduring through difficult times?

Also by Jeff Doles

Personal Confessions from the Psalms
Prayers and Affirmations for a Life of Faith, Happiness and Awe in God

ISBN 978-0-9823536-1-5
5.5 x 8.5 in., 98 pages

Available at www.walkingbarefoot.com

Also by Jeff Doles

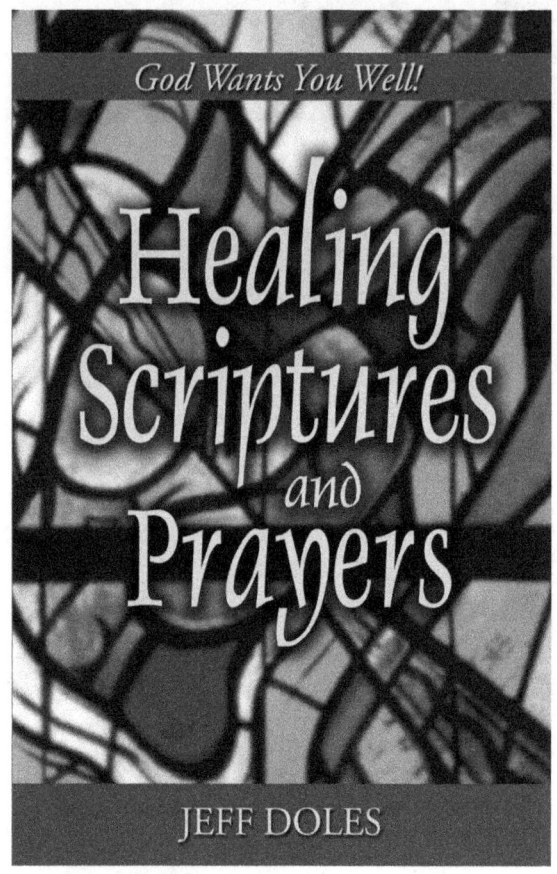

Healing Scriptures and Prayers

ISBN 978-0-9744748-1-6 (Paperback)
6 x 9 in. 120 pages

Available at www.walkingbarefoot.com

Soak in the Healing Scriptures

Vol. 1: Old Testament Scriptures

Vol. 2: New Testament Scriptures

Vol. 3: Healing Names of God

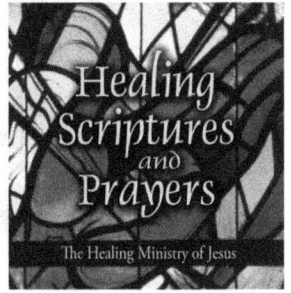

Vol. 4: The Healing Ministry of Jesus

Healing Scriptures and Prayers

Available in CD and MP3
Listen to audio clips and order at
www.walkingbarefoot.com

Also by Jeff Doles

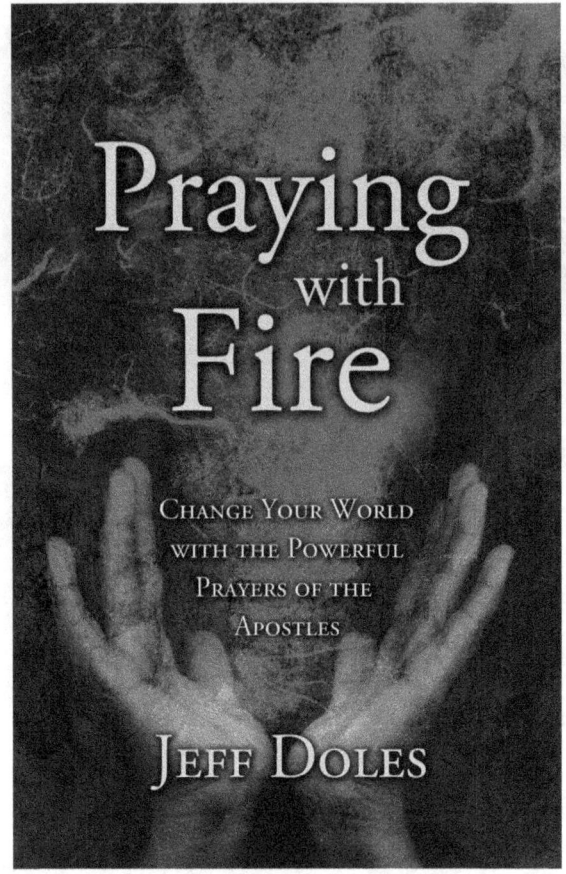

Praying With Fire
Change Your World with the
Powerful Prayers of the Apostles

ISBN 978-0-9744748-6-1
6 x 9 in., 104 pages

Available at www.walkingbarefoot.com

Also by Jeff Doles

Miracles and Manifestations of the Holy Spirit in the History of the Church

ISBN 978-0-09744748-9-2
9.6 x 7.4 in., 274 pages

Available at www.walkingbarefoot.com

Also by Jeff Doles

The Kingdom of Heaven on Earth
Keys to the Kingdom of God in the Gospel of Matthew

ISBN 978-0-9823536-0-8
6 x 9 in., 194 pages

Available at www.walkingbarefoot.com

Also by Jeff Doles

God's Word in *Your* Mouth
Changing Your World Through Faith

ISBN 978-0-9744748-8-5
6 x 9 in., 140 pages

Available at www.walkingbarefoot.com

Also by Jeff Doles

Walking Barefoot
**Living in Prayer, Faith
and the Power of God**

ISBN 978-09744748-0-9
6 x 9 in., 140 pages

Available at www.walkingbarefoot.com

Also by Jeff Doles

From the Manger to the Cross
Advent and Christmas Meditations

ISBN 978-1440427961
5.5 x 8.5 in., 104 pages

Available at www.walkingbarefoot.com

Also by Jeff Doles

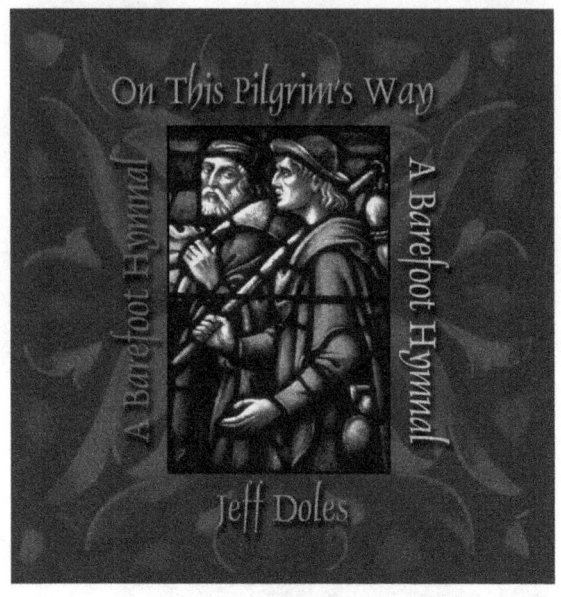

On This Pilgrim's Way
A Walking Barefoot Hymnal

Available in CD and MP3
Listen to audio clips and order at
www.walkingbarefoot.com

Also by Jeff Doles

He Come from the Glory
A Walking Barefoot Christmas

Available in CD and MP3
Listen to audio clips and order at
www.walkingbarefoot.com

www.ingramcontent.com/pod-product-compliance
Lightning Source LLC
Chambersburg PA
CBHW031453040426
42444CB00007B/1086